CRACK IT!

A STUDENT'S PLAYBOOK FOR ACADEMIC AND PERSONAL GROWTH!

N. SATHYANARAYAN

Contents

Contents

Contents

FOREWORD

When Sathya approached me with the idea for this book, I was immediately struck by his passion for empowering students and guiding them toward success. Having been his mentor, business partner, and friend, I have witnessed firsthand his unwavering commitment to helping students navigate the complexities of academic life.

In a world where academic pressure often overshadows personal growth, Sathya has written a book that not only addresses how to prepare for exams but also delves into the holistic development of students. From practical tips on time management to strategies for handling parental expectations, this book is a treasure trove of wisdom for students and their families.

What sets this book apart is its focus on balance—a critical yet often neglected aspect of student life. The chapters explore not just how to study effectively but also how to stay motivated, manage stress, and make informed decisions about one's career path. Sathya's insights, drawn from years of experience, resonate deeply with the challenges faced by Indian students today.

As someone who has spent years working closely with students and parents, I can confidently say that this book is a much-needed guide in the journey toward academic and personal success. Sathya writes with empathy, understanding, and a genuine desire to help students achieve their dreams.

To the readers of this book: approach it not just as a guide to exams but as a companion that will walk with you through one of the most important phases of your life. Use it to navigate the crossroads of education and opportunity, and remember that success is not just about cracking exams—it's about growing into the best version of yourself.

I am proud to endorse this work and hope it finds its way into the hands of every student who seeks clarity, motivation, and success.

— Mohit Mangal

Author and Career Counselor

ACKNOWLEDGEMENTS

This book is the culmination of countless hours of effort, guidance, and unwavering support, and I am deeply indebted to the people who stood by me throughout this journey.

First and foremost, I am eternally grateful to my parents, Narasimhan and Saroja, for their unconditional love, sacrifices, and the values they instilled in me. Your belief in me has always been my greatest strength.

To my wife, Anusha, thank you for your patience, encouragement, and endless support, even during the most challenging moments. Your presence in my life is my anchor.

To my sister, Shweta, and my brother-in-law, Vidyashankar, your constant motivation and words of wisdom have meant more than I can express.

A special thanks to my friend and mentor, Mohit, whose guidance and insights have played a pivotal role in shaping this book. Your wisdom and encouragement have inspired me to push my limits.

I am deeply appreciative of my incredible team at iQue Ideas, whose dedication and hard work have been instrumental in bringing this project to fruition. This book would not have been possible without your efforts.

My heartfelt gratitude also extends to the entire team at Notion Press for their professionalism and support in helping this book come to life.

I would like to extend my heartfelt gratitude to all my cousins, whose names have been used throughout this book for purely illustrative purposes. These references are fictional and by no means reflect any real-life incidents. I deeply appreciate your understanding and good humour in letting me draw upon these names to bring the content to life.

Additionally, I would like to acknowledge the valuable contribution of modern tools like ChatGPT, which supported me in refining ideas, organizing thoughts, and navigating the complexities of writing. Such tools remind us of the power of technology to amplify human creativity.

Finally, to all those who have walked alongside me in this journey, knowingly or unknowingly contributing to this endeavour—thank you. This book is a testament to the power of collective effort and shared dreams.

PART 1: DECISION TIME!

Choosing the Right Stream After Class 10: Science, Commerce, or Humanities? A Guide for Indian Students

Which stream should I opt for, after my std. 10?

I have got great marks in Std. 10. Arts and Humanities are beneath me. I should obviously go for Science.

I am opting for Commerce, as I don't have enough marks to select Science and my marks are not so low that I should take Arts and Humanities.

These are some of the most common phrases that I get to hear from students, who have just completed their Std. 10 and are faced with the decision of choosing a stream for Std. 11 and 12.

For students in India, Standard 10 is a significant milestone. It marks the end of a crucial phase of their academic life and sets the stage for the next chapter: choosing the right stream for Class 11. This decision is not just an academic one; it shapes the entire trajectory of their career and future. It's a question that many students find themselves asking — should I choose science, commerce, or humanities?

While it may seem like a simple decision, choosing between these three streams is far from easy. The choice can feel like standing at a crossroads, each road leading to different opportunities, challenges, and paths. And the weight of this decision is compounded by the fact that it's a decision that will influence the next two crucial years of education and, to some extent, their future career.

It is crucial to make an informed decision when selecting the right stream for you, taking into account your aptitude, interest, personality, and orientation.

The Crossroad: Understanding the Three Streams

Before delving into the specifics of how to choose the right stream, it's essential to understand what each stream entails and the career paths that each can lead to. Let's break it down:

- ✦ **Science**: This stream is often considered the "default" choice for students who have a strong affinity for subjects like Physics, Chemistry, Biology, and Mathematics. The science stream is broad and offers diverse opportunities in fields such as engineering, medicine, research, and technology. But it is also known for its rigorous coursework and demands.

- ✦ **Commerce**: The commerce stream is ideal for students who are interested in the world of business, economics, and finance. It includes subjects like Accountancy, Business Studies, Economics, and Mathematics. Students who opt for this stream often go on to pursue careers in fields like accounting, banking, finance, management, marketing, and economics.

- ✦ **Humanities**: Also known as the arts stream, humanities are the choice for students with a passion for subjects like History, Political Science, Sociology, Psychology, and Literature. It is often seen as the most flexible stream, offering students a wide range of career paths, including law, journalism, design, teaching, social work, and public administration.

For years, the Indian mentality was to hold the Sciences in the highest of regards and Commerce as the subject that one opted for, if they could not make the cut for Science.

Arts and Humanities was sadly treated as the poor cousin and was often considered a sign of poor intelligence and lack of choices.

Thankfully, the scenario is not so bleak in present times. The value of each stream is becoming more apparent by the day. Students (and more importantly their parents) are actively making informed choices.

Let's take a look at some important things to be taken into consideration before deciding on the stream that could potentially set the course for the rest of your adult life.

Step 1: Aptitude – Knowing Your Strengths

The first step in making the right choice is to assess your own strengths. Aptitude, or your natural ability in certain areas, plays a crucial role in determining which stream would be the best fit for you. For example, if you find yourself excelling in subjects like Maths and Physics, and if you enjoy problem-solving and critical thinking, the science stream might be your natural habitat. If you love working with numbers, graphs, and concepts related to business, commerce could be the right choice for you.

On the other hand, if you are someone who finds joy in reading, writing, and debating social issues, the humanities stream may suit you better. The key here is to evaluate which subjects make you feel most comfortable, where you experience success without excessive struggle, and what tasks give you the most satisfaction.

The best way to do this is by reviewing your performance in various subjects up to Class 10. If you consistently perform well in mathematics and science-related subjects, it's a sign that you may be inclined toward the science stream. If you shine in subjects like economics, accountancy, or business studies, then commerce may be a better fit. And if you do well in subjects like literature, history, or sociology, humanities might be your calling.

Step 2: Interest – Fuelling Your Passion

While aptitude is essential, interest is what keeps you motivated over time. After all, you'll be spending a lot of time with the subjects you choose. It's important to think about which subjects truly excite you. The key question to ask yourself is: Which subjects do I find fascinating? Do I enjoy reading about scientific innovations and understanding the world through data? Or do I find satisfaction in reading about human behaviour, history, or political systems?

Interest is often the secret sauce that keeps students going even when the going gets tough.

Students in the science stream often find joy in exploring the mysteries of the natural world, while those in commerce may be passionate about business strategies or financial management. Humanities students, on the other hand, may enjoy discussing societal issues, engaging in debates, and understanding diverse perspectives.

If you find yourself bored by a subject or if it feels like a chore to study it, it's a red flag that you might not be pursuing your true interests. On the flip side, if you eagerly dive into a subject, even in your spare time, that's a good indicator that your interests align with your academic choice.

Step 3: Personality – Understanding Yourself Better

Your personality plays a vital role in determining which stream is best for you. People with different personality traits are often drawn to different fields.

Why does this matter?

Imagine that you study to become a doctor. You excel in academics and gain the best of qualifications. You start your career as a general practitioner. However, you have a rather brusque personality. You cannot be patient with other human beings. You hate interacting with strangers. Do you think, you could succeed as a doctor – a professional, who needs to be calm, caring and patient with strangers, practically every minute of their work life?

On the other hand, you are a gregarious person, a practical joker and a person who is often described as being high on life. Do you think you could manage to work in a role that demands you to be very strict and often curt with your subordinates?

While there is no such thing as a good or bad personality, there is definitely the right personality for the right job.

Let's break this down a bit:

- **Analytical and Logical Thinkers**: If you're someone who enjoys solving problems, thinking logically, and working with numbers, the science or commerce stream might be more suited to you. These streams require a clear, structured approach to learning and often focus on problem-solving and reasoning.

- **Creative and Expressive**: If you're a person who enjoys expressing yourself through writing, arts, and discussions, the humanities stream might be more fitting. Humanities students often thrive in environments where creativity, critical thinking, and self-expression are valued.

- **Practical and Real-World Oriented**: If you're someone who enjoys taking action and applying what you learn to real-world situations, commerce could be a good fit. Students in commerce often engage in practical, business-related tasks and projects, which could appeal to those with a practical mindset.

- **Detail-Oriented and Focused**: If you enjoy digging deep into subjects and finding patterns or connections, the science stream may align with your personality. Science students often need to pay attention to minute details and persist through complex problems.

Step 4: Career Orientation – What Does the Future Hold?

One of the most important aspects of stream selection is thinking about what career you want to pursue in the future. While it's impossible to predict exactly what path you'll take, it's helpful to have an idea of what excites you about the future.

✦ **For Students Who Enjoy Problem-Solving and Innovation**: If you find yourself captivated by technology, medicine, or engineering, the science stream is likely the best option for you. Fields like engineering, medicine, research, and data science require a strong foundation in science subjects like Physics, Chemistry, and Mathematics.

✦ **For Students Interested in Finance, Economics, and Business**: The commerce stream is the ideal choice. Students pursuing this stream often go on to careers in fields like accounting, finance, business administration, marketing, and economics. The commerce stream provides a good foundation for pursuing a variety of professional courses like Chartered Accountancy (CA), Company Secretary (CS), or an MBA in the future.

✦ **For Students Interested in Society, Culture, and Communication**: If you're fascinated by human society, history, and the way people think and behave, the humanities stream is perfect. Students from the humanities often pursue careers in fields like law, public administration, teaching, psychology, social work, journalism, and content writing.

While career prospects are crucial, it's essential to remember that career paths are not always linear. Many students switch careers later on, and the stream you choose in Class 11 doesn't lock you into a single profession for life. However, it's wise to choose a stream that provides a strong foundation for your intended career path.

Step 5: Talking to Mentors and Parents

It's important to seek guidance from mentors and parents when making such a significant decision. Teachers, career counsellors, and parents can provide valuable insights based on their experiences and knowledge of your strengths and weaknesses. Having open and honest conversations with them can help you view the situation from different angles.

However, it's crucial that these discussions don't become overwhelming. The decision should ultimately be based on your interests and aptitude. While the opinions of others are valuable, you should feel empowered to make the decision that feels right for you.

Step 6: Evaluating the Pros and Cons

Every stream has its advantages and challenges. Here's a quick breakdown:

- **Science:**
    - **Pros:** Offers diverse career options (engineering, medicine, research), potential for high-paying jobs, intellectually stimulating.

- **Cons**: Requires intense effort, long hours of study, and a strong aptitude for abstract thinking.

◆ **Commerce**:

- **Pros**: Strong career prospects in business, finance, and economics, options to pursue professional courses like CA, CS, and MBA.

- **Cons**: Can become repetitive, competitive, and can lack the excitement of fields like science or humanities.

◆ **Humanities**:

- **Pros**: Wide variety of career options, flexibility, focuses on creative and critical thinking, socially impactful professions.

- **Cons**: Perceived as less lucrative or prestigious compared to science or commerce, but this is changing rapidly.

Conclusion: Trust Yourself

Choosing the right stream in Class 11 is a decision that requires careful thought, self-awareness, and introspection. It's a decision that will influence not just your academic future, but also your career path. At the end of the day, no one knows you better than yourself. Reflect on your strengths, interests, personality, and long-term goals to make the best decision. Remember, there's no one-size-fits-all answer. Trust your instincts, seek guidance when needed, and choose the stream that will bring out the best in you. The road ahead may be challenging, but with the right stream, it will also be immensely fulfilling.

How to Choose the Right College After Board Exams: A Guide for Indian Students in Std 12 Preparing for Entrance Exams

Which is the best college for me?

How do I select the right college for higher education?

The clock is ticking. For students in India, Standard 12 is a time of intense pressure, as you juggle between board exams, entrance exams, and the looming question that hangs over everyone's head: *What next?* The tension of finalizing your future can feel like a weight on your shoulders, especially when it's time to choose the right college. After years of hard work and anticipation, the decision of where you want to spend the next few years of your life can feel like a monumental one.

Choosing the right college is not just about a prestigious name or rank—it's about finding a place that aligns with your goals, interests, and aspirations.

Let's dive into the factors that matter when selecting a college after your board exams, with a focus on Indian students preparing for entrance exams. We'll talk about everything from understanding your options to weighing the pros and cons of different institutions, all while navigating the pressures and challenges that come with this decision.

The Pressure to Choose the "Right" College

Let's face it—choosing the right college feels like a Herculean task. In a country like India, where the competition is fierce and education holds immense value, every decision feels life-defining. You might have relatives who keep suggesting names of top-tier institutions, friends who are already eyeing their dream colleges, and parents who want to see you settle into a well-paying, respected career. Amid all this external pressure, it's easy to lose sight of the most important factor: *What do you want?*

Most Indian students will be preparing for entrance exams like JEE, NEET, CLAT, or IPMAT, depending on the field they wish to pursue. Whether you're aiming for engineering, medicine, law, or management, the goal remains the same—getting into a college that offers you the best education, opportunities, and environment. But how do you go about selecting the right one?

Step 1: Understand Your Interests and Strengths

Before diving into the intricacies of colleges and entrance exams, the first step in choosing the right college is a little soul-searching. Ask yourself: *What are my interests? What subjects or fields make me excited?*

You've spent the last two years studying hard for your board exams and entrance exams, but deep down, you probably already know what truly excites you. You might have a passion for technology and innovation, which makes engineering the ideal fit. Alternatively, you may have an affinity for understanding human behaviour, making psychology or law an exciting choice. If you're someone who enjoys problem-solving and strategic thinking, a degree in management might be right up your alley.

Choosing a stream and then a college based on your passions rather than external pressure can set you up for long-term happiness and success. Don't just follow the crowd because everyone else is. Remember, "One man's trash is another man's treasure." What excites someone else might not necessarily be your calling.

Step 2: Research and Identify Your Options

Once you've figured out your area of interest, it's time to start narrowing down the list of colleges. This can feel like opening Pandora's box, given the sheer number of colleges in India, but a little research will go a long way.

The first thing to consider is the *field of study* you're interested in. Are you aiming for engineering? In that case, you might focus on colleges like IITs, NITs, or state-level engineering colleges. If you're aiming for medical studies, it would be wise to look into top medical colleges like AIIMS or the state government medical colleges. For law, think about pursuing CLAT and aiming for prestigious national law schools like NLSIU Bangalore or NALSAR Hyderabad. Similarly, for management, institutes like IIMs or Symbiosis are highly sought after.

But don't just stop at the big names. Look beyond the glittering rankings and explore other institutions that offer solid education, excellent faculty, and campus facilities. Researching well will help you build a balanced list of options based on your entrance exam performance and the course that excites you most.

Step 3: Factor in Accreditation and Reputation

In the rush to pick a college, students often overlook the importance of accreditation and institutional reputation. When selecting a college, make sure it is *accredited* by relevant educational bodies such as the University Grants Commission (UGC), All India Council for Technical Education (AICTE), Medical Council of India or the Bar Council of India as applicable. Accreditation ensures that the institution meets academic standards and is recognized by employers, governments, and higher educational institutes.

Moreover, the reputation of a college plays a huge role in your future career. A well-established name can open doors, but don't be swayed solely by brand value[1]. While a top-tier college can give you an edge, a smaller, lesser-known college with strong industry connections or an exceptional faculty can sometimes be more beneficial, depending on your chosen field.

Real-life Example: You may have heard that some smaller institutes are producing top-notch entrepreneurs or researchers in specific fields. Institutes like BITS Pilani or Shiv Nadar University have carved out a niche for themselves despite not being as widely known as the

---

1. Having said this, I have also written about why a Brand name matters. Check out that chapter in this book!

IITs, but they offer excellent opportunities in fields like technology and entrepreneurship.

Step 4: Location, Campus, and Infrastructure

"Out of sight, out of mind." While choosing a college, the location and infrastructure should not be underestimated. You need to think about the place where you'll be spending the next few years of your life. Is the college in a city that fits your lifestyle and career goals? For example, if you're interested in pursuing a career in management, cities like Mumbai or Delhi have a plethora of business opportunities, whereas colleges in tech hubs like Bengaluru and Pune are ideal for tech enthusiasts.

Think about whether you're comfortable with being away from home or if you'd prefer to stay closer. Campus life, facilities, and environment matter too. Does the college offer the extracurricular activities you're interested in? What about hostels, food, and safety? Remember, these little things can make a big difference in your overall college experience.

Step 5: Consider the Faculty and Alumni Network

They say, "The best way to predict the future is to create it." Your professors and mentors are key to shaping your future. A college with experienced faculty members who have expertise in their fields can significantly impact your learning. Research the credentials of the faculty members in your desired department. Are they experienced? Do they have strong connections in the industry? Do they emphasize practical learning over rote memorization?

A solid *alumni network* can also be crucial. Institutions with active alumni networks open doors for internships, placements, and networking opportunities. Many successful professionals have reached their current positions because of the mentorship and opportunities provided by their college's alumni community.

Step 6: Fee Structure and Financial Aid

The cost of education is a significant consideration for many students and their families. College fees can vary greatly from one institution to another, and it's important to weigh the *return on investment* (ROI). While government-funded colleges may have lower fees, private institutions may offer better infrastructure and resources, but at a higher cost. You need to consider whether you're willing to take on a student loan or if your family can comfortably afford the fees.

Additionally, look into scholarships and financial aid options provided by the institution or external bodies. Many colleges offer merit-based scholarships or financial assistance to students who show exceptional promise. Sometimes, a slightly higher fee at a reputed college may be worth the investment, but only if you can manage it financially.

Step 7: Placement and Career Opportunities

After you've put in all the hard work, you want to make sure that your college degree translates into career opportunities. Colleges with strong placement records often have a direct line to top companies looking for fresh talent. Research the *placement statistics* of colleges you're considering. Do they have strong ties with industry leaders? What companies visit the campus for recruitment?

Keep in mind that some courses—like those in humanities or social sciences—may not have the same level of recruitment from big corporates, but they might offer unique opportunities in non-traditional careers. Whether you're interested in law, media, or business management, consider how the college's placement cell can help you get a foot in the door.

Step 8: Trust Your Instincts

At the end of the day, no amount of research can replace your gut feeling. Choosing the right college is as much about *feeling* comfortable as it is about logic. If you visit a campus and feel that it suits your personality, environment, and goals, trust that instinct.

Conclusion: Your Future, Your Choice

Choosing the right college is no easy task. It's about balancing practicality with passion and finding a place that will nurture your dreams while setting you up for success. With entrance exams on the horizon and board exams just around the corner, it's easy to feel overwhelmed by the weight of making the right choice. But take a step back and remember: it's your future, your journey. As long as you align your college choice with your interests, goals, and circumstances, you're on the right track. Whether you end up in a renowned institution or a lesser-known one, what matters most is the effort you put in and the vision you follow.

So, take a deep breath, trust the process, and know that whatever college you choose, you'll make it your own. The path you choose will shape your future—just remember, it's your choice.

Why It's Important to Focus On School Board Exams, Even While Preparing for College Entrance Exams: A Story of Balance, Strategy, and Success

Why It's Important to Focus on School Board Exams, Even While Preparing for College Entrance Exams: A Story of Balance, Strategy, and Success

As the clock ticked closer to the fateful day of his first entrance exam, Avinash sat at his desk, feeling the weight of the world on his shoulders. With books piled high and a notebook brimming with formulas and keynotes, his mind was a whirlwind of equations, reasoning puzzles, and current affairs. Avinash had one dream—to get into one of the prestigious law schools in India. The Common Law Admission Test (CLAT) was his golden ticket, and he was determined to make it happen. But amidst all this exam pressure, there was a nagging thought he couldn't shake off: "What if I don't crack the entrance exam?"

Avinash wasn't alone in this. Across the country, students like him were deep into preparation for various entrance exams—CLAT for law, JEE for engineering, NEET for medicine, CAT for business management, and a host of others for liberal studies, economics, and design. The grind was intense, and it seemed that every waking moment was consumed by thoughts of entrance exams. But there was something more pressing that Avinash's parents and mentors had drilled into him over the years: the importance of the school board exams, the class 12 exams. These exams weren't just another milestone—they were, in fact, a lifeline, the bedrock upon which his future could be built, no matter what.

As Avinash sat in his room, juggling entrance exam preparation and board exam revisions, he couldn't help but wonder: is it really necessary to focus so much on school board exams while preparing for entrance exams? Isn't it enough to just ace the entrance exams? The reality, however, is far more nuanced than it appears. For students like Avinash, focusing on the school board exams—along with preparing for entrance exams—isn't just important, it's crucial for their academic future.

Let's take a deeper look into why this balance matters so much and how it plays a vital role in the college admission process.

The Pressure of Entrance Exams

India's education system is structured in such a way that students face a slew of entrance exams after completing their school education. These exams are perceived as the golden key to the future—a key that opens doors to prestigious institutions in fields like law, business management, medicine, engineering, and liberal studies. As a result, students like Avinash often feel an immense amount of pressure to perform well in these exams. With so much riding on these tests, it's easy for students to put their focus entirely on preparing for them.

Take, for instance, the intense competition for law school admissions. The CLAT, with its thousands of applicants each year, is a make-or-break exam for many aspiring lawyers. Similarly, the JEE and NEET exams for engineering and medicine, respectively, have such cutthroat competition that the difference between success and failure can hinge on a few marks.

While the pressure to excel in entrance exams is undeniable, students must realize that these exams are just one part of the puzzle. The board exams—typically held in class 12—hold significant weight in a student's journey. They can be the deciding factor in college admissions, especially for merit-based systems. So, let's explore why focusing on school board exams is still essential, even in the shadow of entrance exams.

The Role of Board Exams in the Admission Process

In India, not all college admissions are based on entrance exams. Several prestigious universities and colleges still use school board exam marks as a criterion for admission, even for courses like law, business management, and liberal studies. While entrance exams like CLAT, JEE, NEET, and others are required for admission to specific institutions, many universities—especially the ones that don't have their own entrance exams—rely on board exam marks to determine eligibility.

Avinash had spent years hearing about the importance of board exams. His parents, both teachers, often emphasized that the marks obtained in class 12 would play a crucial role in shaping his future. While Avinash was understandably fixated on cracking CLAT, he couldn't ignore the reality that a solid performance in his board exams would serve as a fallback if the entrance exam didn't go as planned. Whether he chose law, business management, or any other course, board exams could be the key to his entry into other institutions that didn't require an entrance test.

Merit-Based Admissions: The Backup Plan

Imagine, for a moment, that Avinash doesn't do well in his entrance exam. The thought felt terrifying, but the possibility was there. If he didn't score high enough in CLAT to secure a seat in a good law school, what would he do? The answer wasn't as bleak as it initially seemed. There were other options—colleges that would base their admissions on the marks obtained in class 12, rather than an entrance exam score.

In fact, this is the case for a significant number of colleges in India. In fields like liberal studies, humanities, and even management, many universities and colleges offer merit-based admission. Many renowned central and state universities rely heavily on class 12 marks for undergraduate admissions. Even some private universities have a similar system, making the board exams an important factor for students looking to secure a spot in their chosen institution.

This is where students like Avinash, who strike a balance between entrance exam preparation and board exam revisions, have an advantage. If one path doesn't work out, the merit-based admission system provides a backup. However, without good marks in the board exams, that backup plan doesn't exist. This highlights the importance of focusing on school exams as a safety net—something that could save the day if entrance exams don't go as planned.

The Overlap Between Board Exams and Entrance Exam Syllabus

One of the major concerns students have when juggling board exams and entrance exam preparation is the overlapping syllabus. Students often feel torn between the two, unsure of how to manage their time effectively. However, there is good news: the syllabus for many entrance exams overlaps with the syllabus of the class 12 curriculum. Whether it's engineering, medicine, business management, or law, the foundation of many entrance exams is built on concepts taught in school.

For example, students preparing for the JEE exam (for engineering) must be well-versed in Physics, Chemistry, and Mathematics—subjects that are also tested in the class 12 board exams. Similarly, students aspiring for NEET (medicine) need a strong grasp of Biology, Chemistry, and Physics, all of which are taught in school.

In the case of law aspirants like Avinash, the CLAT syllabus includes subjects such as English, General Knowledge, Legal Aptitude, and Logical Reasoning—areas that overlap with the subjects, students are already studying in school. By focusing on school exams, Avinash could not only ensure a good score for merit-based admissions but also reinforce his preparation for entrance exams. This overlap makes it possible to study efficiently without completely neglecting one exam over the other.

Avoiding the "All Eggs in One Basket" Trap

One of the biggest mistakes students can make is focusing all their attention on entrance exams at the expense of board exams. This is the proverbial "putting all your eggs in one basket" trap. The logic behind this is understandable—students want to do well in the entrance exams that are seen as the gateway to their dream college. However, relying entirely on the outcome of one exam can be a risky move.

If the entrance exam doesn't go as planned, students are left scrambling, often with no backup plan in place. While entrance exams like CLAT, JEE, and NEET offer a unique pathway to specific courses and institutions, they are not the only path to success. As mentioned earlier, many top-tier colleges still consider class 12 marks for admissions, especially for courses like liberal studies, economics, and business management. Without solid marks in school exams, students may find themselves locked out of these opportunities.

By balancing preparation for both school exams and entrance exams, students ensure that they are not putting all their hopes on one outcome. This balanced approach allows for more flexibility and greater chances of success, whether through entrance exam results or merit-based admissions.

The Stress and Pressure: Striking a Balance

One of the most difficult aspects of preparing for both school board exams and entrance exams is managing stress. The pressure to perform well in both is immense, and students often find themselves feeling overwhelmed. Avinash, like many others, felt the weight of expectations—his own, his parents', and his teachers'. But through this intense period, Avinash learned an important lesson: stress doesn't have to be a burden. It can be a driving force if managed well.

The key to managing the stress is balance. Students must set clear priorities, create a study schedule that accommodates both school exam preparation and entrance exam practice, and make sure to take time to rest and recharge. The fear of failure can be a powerful motivator, but it should not overshadow the need for self-care and mental health.

The Importance of Long-Term Planning

Avinash's story teaches us an important lesson: long-term planning is essential. Students should not view their school board exams and entrance exams as separate entities. Instead, they should recognize that both contribute to the larger picture of college admissions. Planning ahead and ensuring that school board exam preparation is not neglected is critical. This approach not only ensures a good score in class 12 exams but also reinforces a student's ability to excel in entrance exams.

The real secret to success lies in preparation that is consistent, smart, and focused. By creating a schedule that includes time for both school revision and entrance exam practice, students like Avinash can manage the heavy workload and come out on top.

Conclusion: A Path to Success

In the end, Avinash's journey through the whirlwind of school board exams and entrance exam preparation serves as a reminder that both paths—entrance exams and school exams—are important for students in India. While entrance exams are often seen as the key to securing a spot in top colleges, school board exams offer a solid foundation that cannot be ignored. With the right balance, a student can maximize their chances of success, whether through entrance exams or merit-based admissions.

Avinash's story also serves as a cautionary tale for those who put all their eggs in one basket. It's important to remember that life is unpredictable, and the pressure of entrance exams can sometimes lead to setbacks. By focusing on both school board exams and entrance exams, students ensure that they are prepared for any eventuality, giving themselves the best shot at success, no matter which route they end up taking.

At the end of the day, it's about more than just acing exams—it's about preparing for a future where opportunities are plentiful, and dreams are achievable. So, for students like Avinash, it's wise to remember: the school board exams are not just a stepping stone—they are the foundation for everything that follows.

Why Studying from a Branded Institute Matters?

"I am an IITian."

"My daughter is studying at AIIMS New Delhi."

"My post graduate degree is from IIM Ahmedabad."

A huge section of the middle-class families in India give top priority to the education of their children. It is the dream of many parents to see their children as an engineer, a doctor or a chartered accountant. Many students are brought up with the dream of securing admission to an IIT, an AIIMS, an NLU or an IIM. A seemingly disproportionate amount of the family income is often spent on the education of the school going child, in order to ensure that the kid has a decent shot at cracking one of the national level entrance exams and secure a seat at one of the top ranked institutes of higher education. Parents often sacrifice a lot of their time and money to make sure that their child has all facilities required to ease their entry into one of these famous institutes.

The question is, does it really matter?

With the growth and proliferation of social media, it has become common place to see certain celebrities and influencers parody the craze in the minds of parents and children to become an engineer or a doctor, preferably from one of the top ranked national level colleges. There are countless videos of "successful" people who had a bad academic track record, but managed to end up being highly paid individuals. The stories of people like Bill Gates, Mark Zuckerberg and Steve Jobs do the rounds, highlighting how they were college dropouts and yet were highly successful. The apparent moral of these stories is that education is not important. If you have the fire in your belly, nothing can stop you from gaining name and fame.

However, if you pause for a moment and think about it, the number of stories about people who have climbed to the top without a solid foundation in education, is far less than what you be led to believe. What is often missed, is the fact, that the afore mentioned tech billionaires had what it takes to secure admission to some of the top institutions of education. They did not drop out from the local community college. Gates and Zuckerberg are Harvard dropouts. For every one successful college dropout, there are probably a dozen (if not more) success stories of graduates from the hallowed halls of these world class institutions.

For every Gates and Zuckerberg, there are countless Sunder Pichais, Sachin and Binny Bansals, Deepinder Goyals, Narayan Murthys, Nandan Nilekanis, Vinod Khoslas and Raghuram Rajans who have graduated from top institutes.

My point is this, studying at a top-class institution is more likely to set you up for success than not.

Let us try to understand, what benefits can a person get from attending a word class institution. The fact that you will be taught by some of the best minds in the world is a given. However, there are so many other factors that come in to play.

Let's start with the entrance process. In India, it is not child's play to crack a national level entrance examination like the IIT JEE, NEET, CLAT or the CAT. It takes a lot of academic rigor, mental strength, determination, self-confidence and perseverance to be among the few hundreds or thousands to get selected from an applicant pool of probably a few lakh aspirants. The very fact that you are willing to put in the hard work to do what it takes, sets you a step above your peers, who probably did not even start the journey.

The rigorous selection process ensures that a majority of the class that you are going to spend the next few years of your life with, are among the best minds of the nation. Admittedly, the selection process is not 100 percent fool proof. There will be a handful of people in the class, who probably do not match up to the intellectual level of the toppers. There will probably be more than a handful of people who were more deserving than some of the those who were successful in securing admission, and did not make the cut, on account of different factors. But discounting all those, the quality of the student cohort at these top institutions, will still be more than a few notches above those studying in local colleges – no disrespect intended.

When a vast majority of the student population has under gone a lot of disciplined training and probably sacrificed a lot of things in a single-minded pursuit of their goal at a very young age, it can be reasonably expected that the qualities of hard work and discipline become ingrained in their personality. While a few students, who join the top-level institutions, do tend to lose focus on their long-term goals and slack off, the number of hard working, brilliant minds is still significantly large. When you are in a class of 75 percent achievers, you could score a 76 percent and be called the topper. On the other hand, when are surrounded by students who have agonised over losing a single percent when they see a 99 on their mark sheet, you are motivated to give it all that you have to do better. If you have the right attitude, you get motivated to be the la-crème-de-la-crème of your class.

One of the key observations that I have made about the high performing students, is their ability to manage their time well. While students in mediocre institutions moan about the lack of time and their inability to even complete the set syllabus, high achieving students learn to manage their time in such a beautiful manner, that they are able to juggle a multitude of extra-curricular activities, in addition to their regular studies. Take a look at the schedule of students who are doing well at the IITs, AIIMS, NLUs and IIMs. A fair number of these toppers would also be participating in sports, debates, competitions, festivals and more.

How do they manage to do it all?

Well, proper time management has already been mentioned. There are a number of other factors at play. The top-level institutions offer much more than just a good academic education. If you look at the infrastructure and opportunities available at these campuses, you will be left awestruck. I have a theory for this. The students at top level institutes have already proven that they have the academic prowess and the necessary dedication to achieve more than the other students of their age. For an investor, it would be a safer bet to trust this individual to make better use of resources and given better results. In my opinion, this could probably be one of the top factors that motivate companies to give sponsorships for festivals at these top institutions and then visit them for campus recruitment.

For a fresh graduate, there is no indicator of his ability to contribute to the work force, other than the performance that he or she has displayed at college. How do I distinguish between an engineer from an IIT and a local, not-so-renowned Engineering Institute? Can I compare an 80% on the marksheet of an IITian's final year result with an 80% on the marksheet of the local college graduate? In that case, the fact that the IITian has already demonstrated certain superior traits over the other candidate (by cracking an entrance exam which the other person could not) would probably be the only help that I get for recruitment purposes.

Now, it is quite possible that not every graduate from a top institute is necessarily quality material. As a corollary to that, it is also equally possible that I could probably find a top-notch candidate from a relatively unknown college. However, in absence of any specific measurable criterion, how do I make that choice? I cannot afford to gamble. When presented with two candidates with almost identical resumes, with the only difference being that name of the institute from which they have graduated, the safer bet would always be to go in for the higher ranked college.

If all that gyaan does not seem enough, read this.

I was once asked this question on a popular online platform: **How do I keep myself motivated for cracking CLAT?**

I replied:

Imagine this:

A young boy is walking on a public street with his parents. The young boy is in primary school.

The family of three sees a young person coming towards them. This person is wearing the sweat shirt of NLSIU Bangalore.

The parents tap the boy on his shoulder and point towards the sweat shirt clad person. They tell him, "See that person wearing that sweat shirt? That shirt is earned by those who crack an exam like CLAT and secure good marks to make it the top Law School in India. We hope that one day, you will also be like this person and make us proud."

Family friends are over for dinner. They ask the host couple, "So, your child has just completed std. 12. Have you thought about the future?"

The host couple: "Our kid has cracked the CLAT this year. NLSIU Bangalore is the address for our child, for the next 5 years."

The guests: (to their own child) "Wow! See, NLSIU is the best college for law that there is and uncle and aunty are so proud of their child. We sincerely hope that you will take this as a motivational lesson and also study well to get into an equally good college."

When an NLU student (or for that matter, a student of any top college) walks around in public (especially in the college branded sweats), people all around, do turn back to stare (often with envy and respect) at the person who has had the distinction of earning the letters.

So, forget all soppy advice about how studying well will set your career and get you a happy life.

If you want to be the centre of attention among people and want to see them look at you with envy and respect, you need to get into a great college.

For a law aspirant, that means: Cracking the CLAT!

Feel motivated yet?

Dummy Schools: A Shortcut to Failure or a Stepping Stone to Success?

Right off the bat, let me make one thing clear: I hate Dummy Schools. I do not endorse the concept.

Disclaimer 2: I run a coaching centre for under graduate entrance exams.

Now that we have that clear, if you want to know the reasons for my dislike, continue.

First of all, what is the concept of a Dummy School. I speak from the perspective of the Indian School Education System.

In India, a huge number of parents (yes, it is usually the parent rather than the child) who are obsessed with getting their child into a top ranked college for either engineering or medical education. The admission to top colleges in these streams, is usually through some entrance examination. For engineering, we have the Joint Entrance Examination (JEE) while for medicine, we have the National Eligibility cum Entrance Test (NEET).

Theoretically speaking, the student is tested on their knowledge of the school curriculum of specific subjects (usually Mathematics and Science), in these national level entrance exams.

The top scorers in these exams are usually offered a choice of seats in the institutes (in order of merit).

In the initial years, the number of students appearing for the competitive exams were not too high when compared to the number of available seats. The competition was limited. Most students would not need any additional preparation for these entrance exams. The education that they received in a regular school would be more than sufficient to seem through the entrance exam.

Over the years, as the popularity of these courses started wildly growing, the number of seats available grew at a slow pace, while the number of aspirants for these seats, literally exploded! The difficulty level of these entrance exams started getting tougher with every passing year, to be able to reasonable select appropriate candidates for the colleges.

In the current day and age, while there are a few thousand seats available in a particular field, the number of aspirants writing the entrance exams would be in the range of a million or two!

With the increasing level of competition, aspirants would obviously look for gaining an edge over their competitors.

This led to the rise of coaching culture in India.

Bear in mind, during those days, the term 'tuition' and 'coaching' were reserved for those students who were weak in particular subjects, and needed some extra help to cope with their school exams. It was considered a matter of shame, if a student required extra help for school subjects.

Many students would actively try to conceal the fact that they went for extra classes, outside school hours.

Coming back to the topic of coaching for entrance exams; in the beginning, a few teachers started offering specialised coaching, exclusively targeting these entrance exams.

They would focus on making the students rigorously practice for the entrance exams. While some teachers would still emphasis on knowledge acquisition and clarity of concepts, others started teaching to the test. These teachers would focus on strategies to ace the test, with little or no thought to enhancing knowledge. Teach a formula – focus on the what and the how, rather than the why.

Coaching centres started getting a lot of success. With a narrow focus on the entrance exams, students from these institutes started getting admissions to the most prestigious colleges, in large numbers.

Seeing the success of these institutes, a large number of parents started believing that coaching classes were the secret mantra to success.

Enter Economics 101. With a rising demand, coaching classes quickly started cashing in on this opportunity by providing the supply.

They were established as a rapidly expanding business. What was originally a couple of hours of extra teaching, now started mirroring the teaching style of schools. While schools focused on a lot of different subjects, coaching classes started long hour sessions, with exclusive focus on the subjects relevant to entrance exams – and nothing else.

So far so good.

However, now, entrance exam aspirants had to juggle their school timings along with those of the coaching classes.

This led to a serious problem for students. With a limited number of hours available each day, students started feeling the pressure of time.

Parents started questioning the need for formal school education. Does my child really need to attend all those school sessions, where he is taught subjects which are not a part of the curriculum for entrance exams? Can I not just send my child for entrance exam coaching, all day long?

Well, the formal school education boards need a student to have studied in a registered school to be eligible for board exams. The student needs to appear for and qualify in board exams, to be eligible for admission to a college of his or her choice?

How does one get the eligibility for board exams and yet avoid the tedious hours of regular schooling?

Enter – Dummy Schools!

Regular schools require a minimum attendance from the students, in order to allow them to appear for the board exams.

Dummy schools are institutions, where the student enrols himself, and then can conveniently forget about it during the academic year. Attendance policies of dummy schools are a joke. A student gets the necessary documentation, in order to be eligible to sit for a board exam. He can spend all his "productive" hours in a coaching centre and avoid the "hassle" of school education. Why waste time in studying "unnecessary" subjects like languages, arts and crafts, sports etc, when the precious time can be devoted to merely studying maths and science?

After all, the board only needs the student to get a minimum score in each subject, to "pass" that subject. Board exam results are only an eligibility criterion for college admission. As long as the student is above the minimum eligibility threshold, it is only the entrance exam result that "matters".

When this mentality started taking root in the minds of parents and their wards, it is no wonder that dummy schools began to proliferate.

Dummy schools did not have to worry about providing quality education. Hey! They did not even have to worry about providing any education. All they had to do was set themselves up as registered organisations which can enrol students for board examinations, give admission to students, and provide them with the necessary documentation to show them as being eligible for the boards.

Therein lies the problem.

Coaching centres for entrance exams, exclusively focus on the subjects that are relevant for entrance exams. A JEE coaching institute would merely teach Maths, Physics and Chemistry, with focus on the syllabus of the JEE. A NEET coaching centre would focus on Physics, Maths and Biology, with focus on the syllabus of the NEET.

They are not expected to do anything else.

However, is this what we call education?

A narrow focus on things which seem relevant?

Does a formal school education only talk about passing an exam? Board or entrance?

Education does not mean proficiency in a couple of select subjects. School education is supposed to prepare children for life. Formal school education is not just about learning to read and write, Science and Maths.

Valuable life skills, such as communication, team work, social interaction and much more are part of the huge list of skills that children develop while they sit with a bunch of their peers and attend classes. The arts and crafts classes, the group assignments and projects, the school field trips, the cultural festivals, the sports events, the extra-curricular activities – all these play a major role in shaping the child during his formative years and equip him with the skills necessary to thrive in the whole wide world.

If you restrict a child's education to a very limited set of subjects, how do you expect holistic development to take place?

Let us move away from a philosophical sounding argument and look at a cold and practical one.

Does coaching guarantee success in the entrance exam?

As mentioned before, a few lakh students appear for the entrance exams of JEE and NEET every year. There are probably, a few thousand good seats available. Ever given a thought to the vast majority of students who do not succeed in securing admission through the entrance exam?

While coaching centres proudly flaunt their ranks of successful "toppers" across hoardings and advertisements, does any body talk about those thousands of students who did not "succeed"?

Now, consider the case of a student who enrolled himself in a dummy school, in order to "focus" all time, energy and other resources on preparations for entrance exams. The entrance result exams were not in his favour. What does this kid do?

In India, for those colleges that do not grant admission on basis of entrance exams, the board exam results still hold sway. The merit of the student in the board exams plays a vital role in securing admission.

Our student did not fare well in boards. Under the mistaken impression that he just needs to pass the board exams with minimum score to match the eligibility criterion prescribed by the entrance exam, he never focused on "non-essential" subjects – subjects which were not part of any entrance exam, but definitely a part of the boards. After the catastrophic results of his entrance exams, what options is he left with?

It is at this point in time, that we come across a whole host of students and their parents who rue the fact that they fell for the lure of dummy schools.

While people find it easy to dream about positive outcomes and future success, very few have the guts to plan for failure.

A simple what-if analysis can often provide clarity in decision making.

Consider the two courses of action

1. Regular Schooling v.

2. Dummy School

and the two possible outcomes

1. Success in an Entrance Exam v.

2. Failure in an Entrance Exam.

Case 1: Regular Schooling + Success in Entrance Exam

This is great scenario. You have not burdened yourself with any extraordinary coaching. There seems to be no downside to this scenario.

Case 2: Regular Schooling + Failure in Entrance Exam

This is not a great outcome. However, all is not lost. Even if the entrance exam did not work out in your favour, you still have your regular schooling to give you a second chance with board exams.

Case 3: Dummy Schooling + Success in Entrance Exam

This seems like a good outcome. You took a chance and it paid off. To play the Devil's advocate, you sacrificed a lot of regular school experiences and life lessons, in order to start your progress along a specific career path.

Case 4: Dummy Schooling + Failure in Entrance Exam

This is the worst-case scenario. You missed out on a fantastic childhood experience. You may not be well prepared for your board exams. A failure in the entrance exam may seem to leave you with severely limited options for further course of action.

Taking a bird's eye view of the four possible scenarios, regular schooling seems to have far fewer downsides than going with Dummy Schools.

Rest, I leave it up to you.

Should I Take a Drop Year for an Entrance Exam?

I have lost track about the number of times that I have been asked this question by students; both in class and on digital platforms.

What exactly is meant by a drop year, in the context of Indian education?

For school students, the final year of schooling ends with something called the board examination. Whether it be individual state boards on the central board for secondary education, board exams are usually conducted in the months of February – April. Many colleges of higher education grant admissions to students based on their performance in their board exams.

However, many institutes of higher learning grant admissions to students on the basis of some entrance examination, which is separate from the school board exam.

For example, engineering aspirants appear for the Joint Entrance Examination (JEE Mains and Advanced), while medical aspirants appear for the National Eligibility cum Entrance Test. (NEET).

Most students appear for these entrance exams during their final year of school, typically called their 12th Boards.

In India, it is common for students to start preparing for various entrance exams, as much as 3 to 4 years in advance. The craze for these exams is such that many students tend to focus all their time and energy in preparing for them, often at the expense of everything else, including proper preparation for the board exams.

While a select few, manage to crack the exams and secure admission to the institutes of their choice, a vast majority are left out in the cold.

The successful candidates proceed with their further education in the institute of their choice, whereas many students (from the masses) settle for other options.

However, there are a few candidates who believe that their preparation just lacked a little bit more efforts, and given a second chance, they would definitely be successful.

Here comes in the story of the drop year. While some students, who plan to retake the exam, do go ahead with a seat in a less desirable college and prepare for a reattempt, in parallel to their first-year studies at college, a few brave souls decide to risk it all. They decide, not to secure admission in any institute, but devote all their time and energy in preparing for their next attempt. The decision to devote an entire year to exam preparation, instead of taking admission to any institute of higher studies, is called "taking a drop year".

To answer this question, I rely on that age old mechanism, often used by management consultants — a 2 x 2 decision matrix.

My two decision choices are (a) Take a drop and (b) Do not take a drop.

My two possible outcomes are (1) I clear the entrance exam or (2) I do not clear the entrance exam.

Now, let's map each choice with each possible outcome.

1. **Take a drop and Crack the Exam**

   This is a positive scenario. High risk and high return. You consciously took the risk of taking a drop year. If you manage to devote all time, energy and resources to preparing well for the exam, and do get the desired outcome, the drop year would seem to be worth it.

   However, the probability of getting a successful outcome in this scenario is far overshadowed by the possibility of an adverse outcome.

2. **Don't take a drop and Crack the Exam**

   If you decide to go ahead with securing admission to a less desirable institute and yet appear for the entrance exam, along with your first year college studies, the journey is going to be tough.

   On one hand, you will have to manage your time really well. You cannot afford to pay mere lip service to your college studies. You need to consider the possibility that you may not be successful in your reattempt of the entrance exam, in which case, you will have to continue in your less than desirable institute. In this scenario, you cannot afford to not have performed well in your first year of college studies.

   In case you crack the entrance exam, you will need to withdraw your admission from the current institute. This could entail a monetary loss of the college fees that you have paid. While some students may consider it a small price to secure admission in your dream college, considering the considerable cost of college fees, it may not be an easy choice to make for others.

In my opinion, there is a moral dilemma that some students may face. You already secured admission in Institute X, which you will now forfeit, for institute Y.

As most colleges do not fill in seats that go empty, later in the academic year, the seat that you vacated in favour of your dream college, is now wasted. Had you not taken the admission, some other candidate could have secured admission there and completed the course. Are you willing to face this?

3. **Don't take a drop and Don't crack the exam**

This is a less desirable, but relatively safe option.

If you have secured admission to a less preferred college and appear for an entrance exam in tandem, and you do not manage to crack the entrance exam, you are still left with the backup option of continuing with the current college and completing your college education.

This choice leaves with you a disappointing outcome, however, you are not left with nothing.

4. **Take a drop and Don't crack the exam**

This is the nightmare scenario. You take the risk of not securing admission anywhere and planned to spend an entire year's worth of time, energy and resources behind following your dream. Your dream did not materialize. Now what? Do you have a backup option? Your 12th board exam results are already a year old. Will you be able to secure admission to any institute based on your year-old results? In addition, you may have to face the ridicule of society, which does not hesitate in mocking the failure of others.

Whatever be your choice, there are many dilemmas that you will face.

It is up to you to make the right choice.

THE GREAT COACHING DEBATE: DO STUDENTS REALLY NEED TUITION TO SUCCEED?

Short Answer: No

Before I get into any controversy because of this response, give me time to explain my position.

Full Disclosure: I run a coaching centre for under graduate entrance exams of Law, Business Management, Hotel Management, Liberal Studies and Mass Communication among others.

Okay.

Let me first classify coaching into three basic categories:

1. School Coaching

2. Coaching for Specific Aptitude Entrance Exams

3. Coaching for General Aptitude Entrance Exams

School Coaching

Once upon a time, when I was a young boy (my students would visualise a time when Dinosaurs roamed the Earth and I was a prehistoric cave man), tuition classes were not as prevalent as current times, but were slowly picking popularity among the masses. Schools were considered to be the prime location to gain education. There would be a few weak students who were unable to cope up with the teaching done at school and desperately needed some extra attention to understand the subjects and do well in their final exams. For such students, there used to be private tutors. Parents would engage the help of these teachers to help the students understand the subjects better. The concept of coaching as a full-fledged business was not very widely known. Although there were a few brand names established for coaching, they were restricted to specialised coaching for entrance exams such as the IIT and Pre-medical entrance tests.

Tuition classes were considered a mark of weakness. Students who needed some extra help, would go the extra mile to try and hide the fact that they were seeking extra help outside school. However, as I neared the end of my schooling, the popularity of coaching classes started rising. Some schools started getting a bad (often uncalled for) reputation of not being up to the mark when it came to preparing students for the Std. 10th and 12th board exams. It started becoming more common place to enrol students in these tuition classes, along with regular school. Attendance in school was still considered important and tuition classes were give almost the same level of importance. In some places, it was the same set of school teachers who gave tuition classes outside the school hours to students. Some parents started fearing that, if the student did not enrol for the extra classes from the school teacher, their student would not be treated well in school. This fear (true in a handful of cases, unfounded in most) started an era, where enrolling in tuition classes became the rule and not the exception.

In the meantime, the brand recognition of top IITs and Medical colleges started growing. In India, where being an Engineer or a Doctor was always the dream for parents, the value of being an Engineer from an IIT or a Doctor from AIIMS started rising. Some of the initial coaching centres for these exams quickly realised the potential for developing full-fledged coaching centres for their national level entrance exams. Their success with sending a significantly large number of students to these top colleges, fuelled the race to expand their business.

What originally started as a supplementary service to aid the bright few to gain admission in top colleges, soon became a craze among the masses. Parents started believing that while the school education may help students pass the board exams, it was not enough to crack a national level entrance test.

One thing led to the other.

More students started aspiring for the IITs and AIIMS. As the number of applicants grew, the level of entrance exams started getting tougher. As the exams started becoming tougher, the coaching centres started getting validation about their efficacy in being a necessity for cracking the exam.

Traditionally, schools were all about educating the masses. The focus of a good school teacher, remained on making sure that all the students in the class were taught well. Hence, the pace of teaching was often controlled by the slowest learner in the class. On the other hand, the focus on coaching centres was (maybe rightly so) on ensuring that the students cracked the entrance exams. They had to focus on pushing the limits of the students. They could not afford to slow down their pace. This led to a disparity in the level of teaching in schools versus coaching centres. As entrance exams started getting tougher, the school system could not keep up pace. As a result, coaching centres became the preferred medium of education for cracking entrance exams. Slowly, but steadily, the parents of engineering and medical aspirants started focusing on their child's education through coaching centres rather than traditional schools. Things have come to such a state, that the concept of dummy schools have sprouted. Attendance in school is a mere formality. The focus remains on coaching.

Is Coaching Really Necessary for Entrance Exams?

The sun was setting behind the towering buildings of the city as Shweta sat in her room, staring at the pile of study materials that had been accumulating for weeks. The pressure of the upcoming medical entrance exams, NEET (National Eligibility cum Entrance Test), weighed heavily on her shoulders. Her parents, like countless others, had invested not just money, but hopes and dreams into her success. They had enrolled her in one of the most popular coaching institutes in the city, known for its track record of sending students to top medical colleges. Shweta had mixed feelings about the coaching. While she appreciated the structured guidance it provided, she often found herself questioning, "Is this really necessary?" Was coaching the only way to ensure success in such competitive exams, or had it become an unavoidable part of the academic culture in India?

Shweta's story is not unique. Across the country, from the bustling cities to the quieter towns, students preparing for entrance exams such as the JEE (Joint Entrance Examination) for engineering or NEET for medical studies often find themselves enrolled in coaching classes. These institutes promise to provide the best possible preparation, with expert faculty, comprehensive study materials, and a competitive environment. They claim to give students an edge that can help them outshine their peers and secure a seat in top-tier institutions. However, the question remains: is coaching really necessary for entrance exams?

The Rise of Coaching Institutes: The Cultural Shift

In the early years of her school life, Shweta was a bright student. She understood the concepts being taught in class and performed well in her exams. However, as she entered high school, the pressure to succeed started building up. With the increasing competition for seats in prestigious institutions, it wasn't enough to be merely good at school. She was told that to make it to the top, she would need more than just school knowledge. The emphasis shifted to coaching classes, and slowly, a culture began to emerge — one in which coaching became synonymous with success.

Coaching institutes have become an integral part of the educational landscape in India. It's almost as if no student can dream of cracking an entrance exam without enrolling in a coaching program. The reasons behind the rise of coaching institutes are manifold. To begin with, the structure of the Indian educational system plays a significant role in fostering this dependency. The curriculum in schools, especially public schools, often falls short in adequately preparing students for the competitive exams. Teachers, burdened with large class sizes and limited time, may struggle to provide individual attention to students. This lack of personalized focus can lead to gaps in a student's understanding of crucial concepts, particularly in subjects like Physics, Chemistry, and Biology, which are integral to exams like JEE and NEET.

Moreover, the overall motivation in schools can be quite low. Many teachers, often disillusioned by the system, focus on getting through the syllabus rather than ensuring that every student grasps the material thoroughly. This lack of passion among educators, combined with a rigid, exam-oriented system, creates an environment where students feel compelled to turn to coaching institutes for a more comprehensive approach.

The Need for Extra Push: Coaching as a "Necessary Evil"

For Shweta, enrolling in coaching classes seemed like the only logical choice. Her friends, too, were all heading to various coaching institutes in the city, and the fear of being left behind pushed her to join one of the most renowned coaching centers. The teaching was fast-paced, intense, and designed to focus on exam-specific strategies, from mastering multiple-choice questions to solving problems within seconds. It was like a pressure cooker environment, where students were pushed to their limits to perform at the highest level.

Coaching institutes are often seen as a necessary evil by many students. On one hand, they offer structured learning, expert guidance, and intense preparation, which is hard to find in schools. They provide the kind of environment where students can focus solely on their exams, away from the distractions of everyday life. In the midst of a coaching class, there is no room for laziness. Every student is expected to be on their toes, learning, practicing, and revising. This regimented structure creates a sense of urgency that motivates students to perform at their peak.

The irony, however, is that the coaching culture, while providing students with an intense level of preparation, often perpetuates the idea that success is only possible if one attends a coaching institute. This has led to an unhealthy cycle where students believe that if they don't enrol in coaching, they won't be able to compete at the same level as their peers. It is a self-fulfilling prophecy that, once set into motion, becomes difficult to break.

The School vs Coaching Debate: The Dilemma

One might ask, why can't a student simply focus on their school studies? After all, the school curriculum is designed to teach students the fundamentals of various subjects, and the entrance exam syllabus overlaps with what is taught in school. If students were to pay attention in class, stay consistent, and work hard, would coaching still be necessary?

This is where the crux of the matter lies. While the school curriculum provides the basic foundation, it often does not go beyond what is needed for the board exams. The entrance exams, however, require a deeper understanding, problem-solving abilities, and time management skills that are not always cultivated in the school environment. Schools, especially government-run institutions, are often overwhelmed by large class sizes and limited resources, which means individual attention to each student becomes a rare commodity.

On the other hand, coaching institutes focus specifically on the entrance exam syllabus, with expert faculty members who are well-versed in the nuances of competitive exams. They break down complex concepts into digestible parts and teach students how to approach problems strategically, which is crucial for success in exams like JEE and NEET. The exams are designed not just to test knowledge but also to assess how quickly and effectively a student can apply that knowledge under pressure. Coaching institutes help students build that skill by providing mock tests, time-bound assignments, and detailed feedback.

However, the irony lies in the fact that many students attend coaching institutes because they feel neglected or inadequately prepared by their schools. If schools were more proactive in providing comprehensive training and personalized attention, coaching might not be as essential as it is today. The problem, therefore, is not with the lack of coaching itself but with the systemic issues in the education system that push students into a corner.

The Prevalence of the Coaching Culture

The coaching culture in India has become so ingrained that it is now seen as an inevitable part of the educational journey. Parents, too, play a significant role in this trend. The desire to see their children succeed in a fiercely competitive environment has led many to believe that enrolling in coaching institutes is the only way forward. The fear of their child missing out on a top college — and, by extension, a successful career — drives parents to invest huge sums of money into coaching, hoping that it will give their child the edge needed to secure a place in institutions like IITs, AIIMS, or NITs.

The rise of private coaching institutes has created an ecosystem where competition among students is relentless. Everyone wants to be at the top, and coaching institutes often fuel this drive by constantly emphasizing the importance of rankings, scores, and exam results. While this has led to a remarkable increase in the success rates of students from coaching institutes, it has also fostered a sense of fear and anxiety among students who cannot afford or do not attend these institutes.

For Shweta, the pressure was mounting. She had to keep up with the pace set by the coaching classes, attend long hours of extra classes, and study late into the night. She began to wonder whether the constant need to prove herself in such an environment was truly beneficial, or if it was simply adding to her stress and anxiety.

A Systemic Problem: The Need for Reform

At the heart of the coaching culture lies a much deeper issue — the failure of the traditional school system to adequately prepare students for competitive exams. The need for coaching is not because students lack the ability to learn; it is because the education system itself has not evolved to meet the demands of modern competitive exams.

The focus of schools in India has long been on rote learning and exam-oriented teaching, where the goal is simply to pass exams rather than to understand the material deeply. Teachers, especially in government schools, often have to deal with overcrowded classrooms, which makes it difficult to provide individualized attention. Furthermore, the curriculum is outdated, and the emphasis is primarily on board exams, which leaves little room for the holistic development of students.

If schools were to focus more on interactive learning, critical thinking, and problem-solving skills, there would be no need for students to look outside the school system for coaching. However, given the current state of the educational system, coaching has become an unfortunate necessity for students who aspire to make it to the top.

Conclusion: Coaching as a Necessary Evil

The question of whether coaching is really necessary for entrance exams does not have a simple answer. While it is true that coaching institutes provide specialized training, expert guidance, and a competitive environment, they have also become a product of a broken system. The pressure to succeed in India's competitive entrance exams, coupled with the limitations of the school education system, has led to the widespread belief that coaching is essential.

If schools were to provide the right environment, attention, and resources to students, coaching might not be the necessity it is today. However, in the absence of such systemic changes, coaching has become a necessary evil. Students, like Shweta, continue to tread this path, caught between the desire for success and the overwhelming pressure to perform.

In the end, coaching might not be the ultimate answer to cracking entrance exams, but it remains the only solution available in a system that has failed to evolve. While coaching institutes certainly provide value, the real change lies in reforming the school education system — only then will students be able to face competitive exams with the confidence that comes from a strong, well-rounded education.

The Importance of Extra-Curricular Activities for School Children: A Key to Unlocking a Well-Rounded Personality

In the heart of a bustling city in India, there was a school known for its academic excellence. Students from all over the city would flock to this school, hoping to get the best education and secure a future in prestigious universities. Among them was Shruti, a 12th-grade student with dreams of becoming a top-notch lawyer. Like most students, Shruti was focused on excelling in her board exams and preparing for entrance exams. But Shruti was not just another student buried under piles of textbooks; she was actively involved in a variety of extra-curricular activities, from debating to volunteering at local NGOs. This balanced approach to life was what set her apart from many of her peers.

Shruti's journey is a prime example of how extracurricular activities play a pivotal role in shaping a well-rounded personality, especially for Indian students who often face immense academic pressure. While academic excellence is undoubtedly important, it is the skills and experiences gained through extracurricular activities that can give students the edge they need—not only for personal growth but also when it comes to college admissions.

Let us explore why extracurricular activities are essential for school children, especially in the Indian context, and how they contribute to the development of a well-rounded personality. We will also delve into how these activities can significantly enhance a student's chances of securing admission to top colleges and universities.

The Cultural Shift in India: The Rising Importance of Extra-Curricular Activities

Historically, the Indian education system has placed a strong emphasis on academics, often sidelining extracurricular activities as something secondary, or even optional. However, as the country's education system evolves and becomes more competitive, there has been a noticeable shift. In recent years, Indian schools and universities have started to recognize the importance of extracurricular activities in shaping a student's overall personality. The pressure to score high marks in board exams has always been intense, but with the increasing number of students vying for limited spots in prestigious colleges, institutions have begun to value well-rounded students.

Extra-curricular activities have become more than just hobbies—they are now seen as an integral part of a student's academic and personal development. Whether it's sports, arts, music, drama, debate, or community service, each activity helps students discover new interests, develop critical life skills, and create connections that can serve them well in the future. For students in India, especially those preparing for the cutthroat competition of college admissions, participating in extracurriculars can make a significant difference.

Building a Well-Rounded Personality

One of the most significant benefits of extracurricular activities is that they contribute to the development of a well-rounded personality. In a society where academic success often overshadows other aspects of life, engaging in activities outside the classroom can help students strike a balance.

Here's how extracurriculars foster personal growth and personality development:

1. **Building Confidence and Self-Esteem**

   In extracurricular activities, students are often required to step out of their comfort zones. Whether it's speaking in front of an audience during a debate competition or performing on stage during a school play, these activities build confidence. Shruti, for example, found that participating in the school debate competition not only sharpened her argumentative skills but also helped her develop the self-assurance to speak her mind in front of an audience.

   Confidence gained from extracurricular activities can translate into better self-esteem, which is crucial for young students. When they excel in something outside academics, they begin to see themselves as capable individuals, which boosts their overall confidence. This can have far-reaching effects in personal and professional life later on.

2. **Time Management and Multitasking Skills**

In India, where students often juggle multiple responsibilities—preparing for board exams, entrance exams, and attending coaching classes—learning to manage time effectively is crucial. Participating in extracurricular activities forces students to organize their schedules, balancing schoolwork with practices or meetings for their chosen activities.

For instance, Anant, another student in Shruti's school, was an avid player of chess, and his involvement in the school's chess team helped him develop excellent time management skills. Juggling his preparation for engineering entrance exams with regular chess practices taught him how to prioritize tasks and make the most of his time. These skills are invaluable as students transition to adulthood and face even greater responsibilities in college and beyond.

3. **Leadership and Teamwork**

A crucial part of extracurricular activities is the opportunity to develop leadership and teamwork skills. Students learn how to collaborate, share responsibilities, and support their peers in achieving common goals. Activities like sports, school plays, and group projects teach them how to be a part of a team, lead a group when required, and resolve conflicts.

Take Shruti's experience as a member of the school's Model United Nations (MUN) team. As the head of the delegation, Shruti had to lead her team, delegate tasks, and ensure everyone was prepared for the conference. It was a challenging role, but it taught her the value of communication, collaboration, and leadership—skills that she would later leverage when applying for law school. Whether leading a sports team, organizing an event, or coordinating an NGO drive, extracurriculars foster a sense of responsibility that is crucial for personal and professional success.

4. **Enhancing Creativity and Problem-Solving Skills**

Students who engage in creative pursuits such as music, drama, painting, or writing are better equipped to think outside the box and approach problems with innovative solutions. These activities encourage creative thinking, which is often stifled in a traditional academic setting focused solely on textbooks and exams.

When students are given the freedom to explore their creativity—whether by composing a song, acting in a play, or solving complex puzzles—they develop their problem-solving abilities. These experiences help students think critically and approach challenges with a unique perspective, which is a valuable skill both in academics and in life.

The Role of Extra-Curricular Activities in College Admissions

As competition for top colleges in India intensifies, extracurricular activities have become a key differentiator for students. While admission to prestigious institutions like the Indian Institutes of Technology (IITs), National Law Universities (NLUs) and Medical Colleges (AIIMS) depend purely on performance of the students in entrance exams, top business schools, such as the Indian Institutes of Management ((IPMAT @) IIMs), colleges for Liberal Studies (FLAME, PDEU) and others depend not only on academic scores but also on the applicant's overall profile. The extracurricular achievements of a student are often the deciding factor in securing a place in these institutions.

1. **Adding Value to the Application**

   Imagine a student named Vinay, who has done exceptionally well in his board exams and entrance exams, but his application is similar to thousands of others. What sets Vinay apart? Perhaps it's his experience as the captain of the school football team, or his voluntary work at a local NGO, or his exceptional skills in public speaking. These activities add value to his profile, showing that he is not just a bookworm but a well-rounded individual with leadership potential, social responsibility, and a broad range of interests.

   Universities often look for students who not only excel in academics but also contribute to their communities and demonstrate leadership and initiative. An active participation in extracurriculars gives Vinay a well-rounded application, making him stand out in a sea of applicants with similar academic qualifications.

2. **Developing a Personal Brand**

In today's highly competitive academic landscape, building a personal brand is crucial for students. By excelling in extracurricular activities, students can carve out a unique identity that reflects their values, interests, and skills. Whether it's leadership in a sports team, excellence in the arts, or a commitment to social work, these activities allow students to showcase their strengths and passions in ways that go beyond their academic record.

Shruti's active involvement in debating, volunteering, and leadership roles in school allowed her to cultivate a personal brand that aligned perfectly with her ambition to study law. Admissions committees at top law schools look for students who not only perform well academically but also have a track record of engaging with social issues, debating, and making an impact in their communities. Her extracurricular activities, coupled with her strong academic performance, gave her an edge over other applicants.

3. **Scholarship Opportunities**

Many colleges and universities, both in India and abroad, offer scholarships to students who demonstrate excellence in extracurricular activities. Scholarships based on leadership roles, community service, or achievement in the arts and sports can significantly reduce the financial burden on students. These scholarships are often competitive, and students with a rich portfolio of extracurricular activities are more likely to be awarded them.

The Holistic Growth of a Student

In the grand scheme of things, extracurricular activities contribute to the holistic growth of a student. They help shape a student's personality, improve their social and interpersonal skills, and instil values such as empathy, discipline, and teamwork. These experiences foster well-rounded individuals who are not just academically capable but also emotionally intelligent, socially aware, and creatively driven.

When parents push their children solely to focus on academic achievement, they inadvertently neglect the importance of nurturing other facets of their personality. It's not enough to be good at maths or science; a truly successful individual is one who can communicate effectively, work well with others, and lead with empathy. Extra-curricular activities provide the stage for students to showcase their talents, step into leadership roles, and develop life skills that will serve them well in any profession they choose.

Conclusion: A Balanced Approach to Education

Shruti, Anant, and Vinay are just a few examples of how extracurricular activities play an instrumental role in shaping a student's academic and personal life. As competition for college admissions continues to soar, students who participate in extracurriculars are more likely to develop a well-rounded personality, build a strong application, and stand out in a crowd of academically accomplished peers.

While academic excellence is undeniably important, it is the skills, experiences, and character developed through extracurricular activities that make a student truly exceptional. These activities allow students to step out of their comfort zones, discover new passions, and prepare for the challenges that lie ahead. The future belongs to students who not only excel in the classroom but also possess the leadership, creativity, and social responsibility to make a meaningful impact in the world.

As the saying goes, "All work and no play makes Jack a dull boy." In the context of today's fast-paced, competitive world, extra-curricular activities provide the perfect antidote to academic monotony, offering students the opportunity to grow, learn, and shine in ways they never thought possible. For Indian students, especially, these activities are not just important—they are essential.

PART 2: PREPARING FOR EXAMS

THE GOLDEN RULES OF STUDYING: A GUIDE FOR INDIAN SCHOOL STUDENTS

What are your top 5 rules of studying?

1. Study quality, not quantity.

2. Study to understand - not just to score marks.

3. Never stop till the concept is clear - which means, once learned, it never has to be done again.

4. Study regularly - never at the last moment. The 24 hours before a test must be free.

5. Teach someone if you can. It helps clarify concepts

In a country like India, where education is highly valued, students often find themselves grappling with enormous expectations and intense competition. From preparing for board exams to entrance exams, the pressure to perform can weigh heavily on young shoulders. However, in this race for academic success, students frequently fall into the trap of simply focusing on completing their syllabus, spending long hours poring over textbooks, without considering the quality of their study sessions.

The truth is, there's more to studying than just putting in long hours. Smart studying can make all the difference between success and burnout. In this article, we'll delve into the **five golden rules of studying** that every student should follow to maximize their learning potential. These rules are not only applicable to Indian school students but can be useful for anyone striving for academic excellence while maintaining mental well-being.

1. **Study Quality, Not Quantity**

    It's an age-old debate: *Is it better to study for 8 hours straight or to study for 4 hours with intense focus and understanding?* The answer is clear – quality matters far more than quantity. It's tempting to believe that the longer you study, the better your chances are of succeeding. But the reality is that long hours of studying without focus can often lead to diminishing returns. It's like trying to fill a bucket with water that has a hole in it. No matter how much effort you put in, the water just slips away.

    Students in India often have a tendency to measure their academic progress based on the sheer number of hours spent studying. But research shows that long hours of studying with distractions and fatigue don't lead to better learning. In fact, they can lead to burnout and reduced retention. Instead, focus on the quality of your study sessions. One hour of focused, uninterrupted study will likely be more effective than three hours of distracted, half-hearted cramming.

The key to achieving high-quality study sessions is to find your most productive time of day. Some students are naturally morning people, while others are night owls. Identify when your concentration is at its peak and align your study schedule accordingly. Also, use tools like the Pomodoro Technique to manage your time effectively. This method involves studying for 25 minutes and then taking a 5-minute break. After four cycles, take a longer break to recharge.

Lastly, ensure your study environment is free from distractions. A clutter-free, quiet study space can make a world of difference in your focus and productivity. With quality over quantity, you'll get much more out of your study sessions and save yourself from the exhaustion that comes with long, unproductive hours.

2. **Study to Understand, Not Just to Score Marks**

One of the most common mistakes that students make is treating studying as a mere means to score marks rather than to understand the subject matter. It's not uncommon for Indian students, especially those preparing for board exams or entrance exams, to cram information into their minds without taking the time to understand it. The focus is on memorizing answers and formulas, often at the expense of genuine comprehension.

While scoring well is important, the true value of studying lies in understanding the concepts. Think about it – when you understand something, you don't just memorize it; you internalize it. This makes it easier to recall information in a variety of contexts, and more importantly, it helps you apply your knowledge in real-world situations.

For example, if you're studying physics, rather than memorizing the formulas, focus on understanding how they are derived and how they apply to real-life problems. Ask yourself why a particular concept works the way it does. If you're studying history, instead of rote-learning dates, try to understand the context behind events, the causes, and the effects. This will help you retain the information in a way that goes beyond mere memorization and prepares you for application-based questions.

One of the most effective ways to encourage understanding is to take an active approach to learning. Rather than passively reading or highlighting your textbooks, try to explain the concepts to yourself out loud or write them in your own words. When you can articulate an idea clearly, it's a sure sign that you've truly understood it.

In India, students are often under immense pressure to perform well in competitive exams, and this can lead them to fall into the trap of learning only what's necessary for the exam. But real success lies in mastering concepts, not just answering exam questions. When you focus on understanding rather than memorizing, you will have a much better chance of not only doing well in exams but also excelling in your chosen field later in life.

3. **Never Stop Till the Concept is Clear – Once Learned, Never to be Done Again**

Have you ever found yourself revisiting the same concept over and over again because you just couldn't grasp it? Many students, especially in India, often get frustrated by topics that seem difficult to understand at first. The temptation is to skip it and move on to the next chapter or subject, hoping that the answer will somehow come to you later. However, this is a mistake. The golden rule here is: *Never stop till the concept is clear.*

When you're studying, don't let confusion fester. If you come across a concept that seems unclear or difficult, take the time to fully understand it before moving on. The longer you leave a concept unaddressed, the harder it will become to understand it later. In fact, this could snowball into a cycle of confusion and frustration. Instead, deal with it head-on. Use online resources, consult your teachers or classmates, or refer to additional books to clarify the topic.

Once you've mastered a concept, don't revisit it repeatedly unless necessary. By fully understanding the topic once, you won't need to waste time going over it again and again. It will be firmly entrenched in your memory, making it easier to recall when required.

A real-life example of this can be seen in subjects like mathematics, where one concept often builds upon another. If you don't understand algebra, it will be hard to understand calculus, and so on. The same goes for subjects like chemistry and physics, where foundational concepts are crucial for tackling more advanced topics. By ensuring you never move on without clearing your doubts, you are building a strong foundation for your studies, and that pays off in the long run.

4. **Study Regularly - Never at the Last Moment. The 24 Hours Before a Test Must be Free**

Ah, the dreaded last-minute cramming! We've all been guilty of it at some point in our academic lives. It's easy to fall into the trap of thinking that you can leave your preparation until the last few days or even hours before the exam. However, this is a surefire way to experience stress and disappointment. The 24 hours before an exam should be reserved for relaxation and revision, not frantic last-minute studying.

The secret to doing well in exams is consistency. Studying regularly, day by day, ensures that you don't have to cram and that your mind is fresh when exam day arrives. When you make studying a part of your daily routine, you build up your knowledge gradually, allowing it to sink in and become part of your long-term memory. This approach reduces the need for high-pressure, last-minute study sessions and helps reduce stress.

Regular study also allows you to identify any weak areas long before the exam. If you notice that you're struggling with a particular topic, you have enough time to work on it, rather than being caught off guard the night before the exam.

In India, students often fall into the trap of last-minute cramming due to the pressure of competitive exams and the volume of material they have to cover. But, remember: *the more you practice, the less you have to perfect at the last minute.* Developing a study schedule early on and sticking to it ensures you don't find yourself in a mad scramble as exams approach.

5. **Teach Someone if You Can. It Helps Clarify Concepts**

One of the best ways to ensure you've truly understood a concept is to teach it to someone else. The saying "To teach is to learn twice" couldn't be more accurate. Explaining a concept to another person forces you to simplify your understanding and fill in any gaps in your knowledge. It also helps solidify the information in your own mind.

In India, students often study in groups, and this can be a great way to reinforce your learning. If you're studying for exams with friends or classmates, take the time to explain concepts you've mastered. When you explain a concept out loud, you not only help others but also clarify your own understanding. Teaching someone forces you to think critically about the topic and connect ideas in a way that helps you retain the information better.

Sometimes, teaching someone else reveals aspects of the topic you hadn't fully understood, and that's when the learning truly happens. So, don't hesitate to explain what you know. Whether it's a peer or even a younger sibling, teaching can be a powerful tool in ensuring that you grasp the material.

Conclusion

Studying isn't just about the hours you put in; it's about how effectively you use that time. The golden rules of studying—studying with quality, understanding concepts rather than memorizing them, not stopping until you truly understand, studying regularly, and teaching others—can make all the difference in your academic success.

In India, where students often face overwhelming pressure to succeed in board exams and competitive entrance exams, these principles can provide a framework for reducing stress and maximizing learning potential. By following these rules, students can ensure they are not just preparing for exams but truly mastering the material.

On the Role of Self-Study vs Coaching in Exam Success: A Deep Dive for Indian Students in Std 12

In India, the journey through Class 12 is often seen as one of the most crucial years of a student's academic life. It's a time when the results of board exams and entrance exams determine the course of a student's future. Every student in Class 12 dreams of making it to a prestigious college, whether it's for engineering, medical, law, business management, or liberal studies. The question that often weighs heavily on their minds is: **"Should I rely on self-study, or should I go for coaching?"**

The debate between self-study and coaching is as old as time, especially in India, where competitive exams are a major part of the academic culture. Each student must find a strategy that works best for them, balancing the pressure to perform with the need to maintain a healthy mental and emotional state. In this chapter, we'll explore the pros and cons of both self-study and coaching, how they impact student performance, and how students can strike the right balance to maximize their chances of success.

The Pressure Cooker Environment: An Overview of Indian Education System

Before delving into the comparison of self-study versus coaching, it's important to understand the environment in which Indian students are preparing for their exams. In India, students in Class 12 often face immense pressure to perform well academically. The stakes are high. Entrance exams like JEE (Joint Entrance Examination), NEET (National Eligibility cum Entrance Test), CLAT (Common Law Admission Test), and others, add a layer of complexity. While these exams determine admission to top colleges, they also open doors to careers that promise financial stability, prestige, and job security.

This pressure to succeed creates a culture of extreme competitiveness, which in turn influences students to look for the most effective ways to prepare. Some believe that self-study is the way to go— after all, it's free, flexible, and independent. Others argue that coaching provides the structured environment and expertise needed to crack tough exams. This divide has sparked debates for years, with both sides presenting strong arguments.

Self-study: The Path of Independence

Self-study is a method where students take charge of their own learning without formal guidance or structured programs like coaching. It's a way for students to develop independence, discipline, and self-reliance. In India, many students prefer this method due to its cost-effectiveness and the freedom it offers. But, just like a coin with two sides, self-study has its pros and cons.

Pros of Self-study

1. **Cost-Effective**

   The biggest advantage of self-study is that it's free. Students don't have to pay for coaching fees, study materials, or tuition classes. In a country where the cost of coaching institutes can be prohibitive for many families, self-study provides an economical alternative.

2. **Flexibility and Autonomy**

   Self-study offers flexibility in terms of time management. Students can create their own study schedule and choose the pace that suits their learning style. For instance, if they feel confident in a particular subject, they can move on to something more challenging without feeling rushed by the set curriculum of coaching classes. This flexibility is crucial for students who work better without external pressure.

3. **Deeper Understanding and Self-Motivation**

   When students engage in self-study, they often develop a deeper understanding of concepts. They are not spoon-fed information but are forced to figure things out on their own. This can lead to a greater sense of accomplishment and boosts self-confidence. Moreover, self-study helps build time-management and problem-solving skills, which are invaluable in the long run.

4. **Personalized Learning Experience**

   Every student is different. Some may grasp a concept in an instant, while others may need more time. Self-study allows students to personalize their learning experience. They can dedicate more time to subjects or topics they find difficult and spend less time on areas where they excel. This individualization allows for a focused approach to mastering the syllabus.

Cons of Self-study

1. **Lack of Expert Guidance**

   One of the biggest challenges of self-study is the lack of expert guidance. While students may have access to books and online resources, they don't have the benefit of a teacher to clarify doubts or offer insights that only come with years of experience. Sometimes, students may misunderstand or misinterpret concepts, which can lead to confusion and setbacks.

2. **Motivation and Discipline Issues**

   It's easy to procrastinate when you don't have someone pushing you. Self-study demands a high level of motivation and discipline. Without the structure of regular classes or the accountability that comes with coaching, many students find it hard to stay on track. The lack of routine can result in gaps in knowledge or even burnout due to overwork.

3. **Overwhelming Amount of Content**

   The Class 12 syllabus for school board exams and competitive exams is vast and can be overwhelming. Students who choose self-study often face the problem of not knowing where to start or how to approach the entire syllabus. Without external guidance, they may also fail to prioritize important topics for entrance exams, which can lead to incomplete preparation.

4. **Lack of Peer Interaction and Competition**

   Self-study can be isolating. Students may miss out on the benefits of interacting with peers who are also preparing for exams. The competitive spirit and healthy discussions that arise in group study sessions are often absent. This can make the preparation process feel lonely and less engaging.

Coaching: The Structured Approach

On the other hand, coaching is a method where students receive professional guidance from teachers or coaching institutes. These institutes offer structured programs designed to help students succeed in both board exams and competitive exams. Coaching is particularly popular among Indian students preparing for entrance exams like JEE, NEET, and CLAT. Let's take a look at the advantages and disadvantages of coaching.

Pros of Coaching

1. **Expert Guidance and Experience**

   One of the key benefits of coaching is the access to expert guidance. The instructors in coaching classes are usually subject-matter experts who have years of experience and know the ins and outs of the syllabus. They help students understand difficult concepts, offer shortcuts for problem-solving, and provide valuable exam tips. This expert knowledge can make a world of difference, especially when students are preparing for highly competitive exams.

2. Structured Learning Environment

Coaching institutes provide a well-organized structure for exam preparation. The syllabus is broken down into manageable portions, and a timetable is set to ensure that all topics are covered before the exam. This structure can be highly beneficial for students who struggle to plan their own study schedules or lack the self-discipline to stay on track. Moreover, coaching helps students manage both school board exams and entrance exams without missing out on critical topics.

3. Regular Mock Tests and Practice

Coaching centers are known for conducting regular mock tests and practice exams. These simulate real exam conditions and help students gauge their preparation level. Mock tests are particularly valuable as they expose students to the exam format, time constraints, and difficulty level. They also help identify weak areas that need improvement.

4. Peer Learning and Motivation

In a coaching class, students are surrounded by peers who are going through the same journey. This creates a sense of camaraderie and healthy competition. Peer discussions and group study sessions allow students to exchange ideas, clarify doubts, and motivate each other. This group dynamic can help students stay focused and on track with their preparation.

5. **Accountability and Time Management**

The regular classes and assignments in coaching provide a sense of accountability. Students know that they are expected to complete assignments, attend classes, and take tests. This built-in routine forces them to stay disciplined and committed to their studies, helping them manage their time effectively.

Cons of Coaching

1. **High Cost**

One of the major drawbacks of coaching is the cost. Coaching classes, especially those that offer personalized or intensive programs, can be expensive. The fees for reputed institutes can run into thousands of rupees, making it unaffordable for some families. For many students, the pressure to succeed in these expensive courses adds to the financial strain.

2. **Less Flexibility**

Unlike self-study, coaching offers less flexibility in terms of study hours and schedule. Students must attend classes at fixed times and follow the pace set by the instructor. This can be challenging for students who prefer studying at their own pace or need more time on certain topics. Additionally, students who are already overwhelmed with school assignments may struggle to manage the additional burden of coaching.

3. **One-Size-Fits-All Approach**

While coaching offers expert guidance, it is often designed to cater to the needs of a large group of students. As a result, it may not provide the personalized attention that some students need. Those who struggle with certain concepts may feel lost in the crowd and unable to catch up. Coaching institutes are not always equipped to cater to individual learning styles, which can be frustrating for some students.

4. **Overdependence on Coaching**

    A common pitfall of coaching is that students may become over-reliant on external guidance and stop taking ownership of their learning. Instead of supplementing their own study efforts, students may depend too heavily on coaching for all the answers, which can limit their ability to think critically and solve problems independently.

Striking the Right Balance: Self-study + Coaching

While both self-study and coaching come with their own set of benefits and drawbacks, the key lies in finding a balance between the two. For many students in Class 12, combining self-study with coaching is the ideal approach.

✦   **Use Coaching as a Foundation**

    Students can use coaching to build a solid foundation of concepts and strategies. Once they have mastered the basics with the help of expert guidance, they can shift to self-study for deeper understanding, additional practice, and personal revision.

✦ **Time Management is Key**

The trick is to manage time effectively. Students should attend coaching classes, but also make sure to allocate sufficient time for self-study. Creating a study timetable that includes both coaching assignments and independent study hours can help ensure that all areas are covered.

✦ **Use Coaching to Fill Gaps**

Coaching can help fill gaps in knowledge and provide valuable exam strategies, but students should not treat coaching as a substitute for self-study. Self-study helps develop the critical thinking and problem-solving skills needed for success, and coaching can't teach that.

✦ **Prioritize Mental Health**

It's important to maintain a balance between academic pressures and mental health. Whether a student opts for self-study, coaching, or a combination of both, ensuring that they have time for relaxation, hobbies, and social activities is crucial.

Conclusion

The debate between self-study and coaching will continue to persist for years to come. Both methods have their strengths and weaknesses, but ultimately, the success of a student depends on how well they can integrate both approaches into their exam preparation. Self-study offers independence, cost-effectiveness, and flexibility, while coaching provides expert guidance, structured learning, and peer motivation.

For students in Class 12 preparing for both board exams and entrance exams, the key is finding the right balance. Embrace the best of both worlds—use coaching for structured learning and expert support, and use self-study to personalize your learning experience and take ownership of your success. No matter which path you choose, the ultimate goal is to stay focused, stay disciplined, and most importantly, stay motivated.

Maximizing Performance in Objective Type Questions: A Guide for Indian Students in Std 12

As you prepare for entrance exams, one thing becomes clear—objective-type questions are a significant part of almost every exam in India. Whether you're preparing for engineering (JEE), medical (NEET), law (CLAT), or business management entrance exams, objective questions form the crux of the assessment. These questions, though straightforward, can be a double-edged sword. On one hand, they offer a quick way to test your knowledge; on the other, they come with the challenge of being tricky and requiring speed, accuracy, and strategy.

For students in Class 12 in India, the pressure to perform well in these exams is immense. With high stakes and fierce competition, maximizing your performance in objective-type questions can make or break your future. The good news is that with the right strategies, you can increase your chances of performing well and ensure you don't fall into the traps set by tricky multiple-choice questions (MCQs).

Let's delve into some essential tips and tricks that will help you maximize your performance in objective-type exams. These strategies, when put into practice, will not only help you ace the exams but will also provide you with the confidence to handle those seemingly complex MCQs.

1. **Understand the Pattern of the Exam**

   The first step in maximizing your performance in objective-type questions is to understand the exam pattern. Each entrance exam, be it for JEE, NEET, CLAT, or any other competitive exam, has a specific format. The types of questions, the time allotted, and the number of choices for each question can vary.

   For instance, in JEE, NEET, or CLAT you might face questions that have four-five options, one of which is the correct answer. Negative marking might come into play for incorrect answers. Before you start your preparation, it's crucial to go through previous years' question papers and familiarize yourself with the pattern.

   Why is this important? Understanding the exam pattern allows you to strategize. You'll know if you need to prioritize accuracy (in exams with negative marking) or if you can afford to guess some questions. It also helps you get comfortable with the timing—how long you can afford to spend on each question and when to move on.

2. **Focus on Conceptual Clarity**

   Objective-type questions are designed to test not just rote memorization but also your understanding of concepts. The key to performing well in MCQs lies in having a solid grasp of the core concepts. When you're studying, make sure that you don't just memorize formulas or facts; understand the "why" and "how" behind them.

For example, in physics, don't just memorize the formulas for motion, work, or energy. Understand the principles behind these formulas and how they apply to different situations. The better your conceptual understanding, the easier it becomes to eliminate wrong choices in an MCQ.

Tip: If you find yourself memorizing without understanding, take a step back. Go through your textbooks or watch online tutorials to break down complex concepts into simpler pieces. As they say, "A clear foundation builds a strong structure."

3. **Practice, Practice, and More Practice**

The most effective way to excel in objective-type exams is practice. It's the difference between knowing the concept and knowing how to apply it under exam conditions. The more you practice, the more you'll improve your speed and accuracy, which are key in MCQs.

- **Daily Practice:** Set aside dedicated time each day to solve objective-type questions. Start with questions that test basic concepts and gradually move on to more advanced ones.

- **Mock Tests:** Taking full-length mock tests under exam conditions is a game-changer. It gives you a taste of the real exam environment, helps you manage your time effectively, and improves your stamina for the actual test.

♦ **Review Your Mistakes:** After every practice session, go back to the questions you got wrong. Understanding why you made a mistake helps you avoid repeating it in the future. It's crucial to learn from your mistakes and improve.

Remember, as they say, "Practice makes perfect." The more problems you solve, the sharper you get.

4. **Time Management: The Clock is Ticking**

One of the biggest challenges of objective-type exams is time management. The clock is ticking, and you need to balance speed with accuracy. Sometimes, the difference between a correct answer and a wrong one lies in the ability to answer quickly without sacrificing precision.

Here are a few tips to manage your time better:

♦ **Prioritize Easy Questions:** Start with questions that are easy for you. Answer them quickly to build confidence and gain momentum. This also frees up time for more difficult questions.

♦ **Avoid Sticking to One Question:** If you're stuck on a question, don't waste too much time on it. Mark it for review and move on. If you have time left over, go back to those tricky questions later.

- **Set Time Limits:** Practice solving questions within a fixed time limit. This will help you pace yourself during the actual exam and avoid spending too much time on one question.

- **Use Elimination Strategies:** Sometimes, it's quicker to eliminate the wrong answers than to try and figure out the right one. Even if you're unsure, eliminating two options can significantly increase your chances of guessing the correct answer.

Time management isn't just about working quickly—it's about working smart.

5. **Master the Art of Guessing (When Necessary)**

Objective exams often leave you with a tough choice: should you guess the answer or leave it blank? In exams with negative marking (such as JEE, NEET or CLAT), guessing can be risky. But there are ways to improve your odds of guessing correctly.

- **Eliminate Obvious Wrong Answers:** When faced with an uncertain question, always eliminate the answers that you know are definitely wrong. This will increase your chances of guessing the right answer.

- **Look for Patterns:** Sometimes, you'll notice that certain options tend to appear more frequently than others. This might be a useful tool when guessing.

- **Use Logical Deduction:** Some questions, even if you don't know the exact answer, can be logically deduced based on the principles you've learned. For example, in chemistry, balancing equations or understanding molecular structures can often help you figure out the right answer.

But remember, "A guess is never a replacement for solid preparation." Guessing should only be your last resort.

6. **Focus on Shortcuts and Formulas**

In subjects like mathematics, physics, and chemistry, where calculations are key, knowing shortcuts and important formulas can save you time. Being able to quickly apply a formula or recognize a pattern allows you to complete problems faster.

Here's how to use shortcuts effectively:

◆ **Create a Formula Sheet:** Write down all the important formulas and concepts on a sheet of paper. Revise this sheet regularly, especially as your exam draws closer.

◆ **Memorize Key Concepts and Steps:** Certain types of problems, such as solving quadratic equations or using Newton's laws in physics, often require following a series of steps. Memorize these steps so that you can quickly implement them under exam conditions.

Tip: Knowing the shortcuts and formulas gives you an edge over students who might be fumbling for the right approach during the exam.

7. **Stay Calm Under Pressure**

Finally, perhaps the most important strategy for maximizing performance in objective-type exams is maintaining a calm and composed mindset. Anxiety and panic can cloud your judgment and lead to careless mistakes.

♦ **Breathe Deeply:** Before you begin the exam, take a few deep breaths. This helps relax your mind and body, allowing you to focus better.

♦ **Stay Positive:** Keep a positive attitude throughout the exam. If you don't know the answer to a question, move on. Don't let it affect your confidence for the rest of the exam.

♦ **Trust Your Preparation:** You've worked hard to prepare for this moment. Trust yourself, and approach each question with a calm and analytical mindset.

"Keep calm and carry on"—this simple mantra can make a world of difference.

Conclusion: The Road to Success in Objective Exams

Maximizing performance in objective-type questions requires a mix of smart strategies, efficient time management, and a calm mindset. By focusing on conceptual clarity, regular practice, and strategic guessing, you can significantly boost your chances of doing well in entrance exams. But remember, the key to success lies not in simply solving questions; it's about doing so efficiently and accurately, without succumbing to pressure or overthinking.

For students in Std 12 preparing for entrance exams, it's a long road ahead, but with the right tools and techniques, the journey becomes a little easier. As the exams approach, stay focused, stay calm, and trust in the preparation you've put in. After all, hard work and smart strategies always pay off in the end.

Why It's Wise to Appear for More than One Entrance Exam for College Admission: A Story of Opportunities and Strategy

As the sun rose over Vijay's small town in Uttar Pradesh, he felt a mixture of excitement and nervousness bubbling inside him. The day was fast approaching—the day he would sit for the Common Law Admission Test (CLAT), the entrance exam that could shape his future. He had been preparing for months, burning the midnight oil, memorizing legal terms, practicing reasoning skills, and revising English grammar. But there was still something that gnawed at the back of his mind—was CLAT the only path to his dream of studying law?

Vijay's friends were in a similar predicament. Some were gearing up for the CLAT, while others were focused on the Symbiosis Law Admission Test (SLAT). There was a handful of students who also had their eyes set on the Common University Entrance Test (CUET) entrance exams, while a few others were considering options outside law altogether, like the Integrated Program in Management Admission Test (IPMAT) test for management schools or the entrance exams for liberal arts colleges.

Vijay's story is not unique. Every year, thousands of students in India sit for numerous entrance exams for college admissions. These exams—ranging from law, management, and liberal studies to engineering and medical fields—are often the gateway to a student's future. While some students put all their eggs in one basket, focusing on a single entrance exam, others, like Vijay, understand the value of appearing for multiple tests. But why is it so wise to do so? What makes it advantageous to take the risk and prepare for more than one entrance exam? Let's dive into Vijay's journey and explore why, for students like him, appearing in more than one exam is a strategy that pays off.

The Myth of the Single Entrance Exam

In India, many students still believe that the key to success lies in a single, well-prepared entrance exam. The thought process is simple—one test, one goal, one success. For students pursuing law, for example, they often focus all their energy on preparing for the CLAT, the most widely recognized entrance exam for law schools in India. Similarly, students interested in management focus on the Common Admission Test (CAT) for admission to post graduate courses at prestigious Indian Institutes of Management (IIMs).

While this approach might work for some, it can also be a double-edged sword. After all, a lot can go wrong when you bet all your future on one exam. Vijay knew this well. Even though he was giving his best shot at CLAT, he also realized that it might not be the only route to success.

The Power of Multiple Paths

The truth is that college admissions in India are not limited to a single exam. While some prestigious institutions are known for their rigid selection processes, many others offer diverse opportunities. Law students, for example, can apply to multiple universities with different entrance exams, such as CLAT, AILET (All India Law Entrance Test), and the CUET exams. Post graduate management aspirants have the option to consider CAT, XAT (Xavier Aptitude Test), SNAP (Symbiosis National Aptitude Test), and MAT (Management Aptitude Test). Liberal studies candidates can opt for the DU entrance exams, IP University's CET (Common Entrance Test), or other university-specific tests.

Vijay understood that having multiple exams lined up meant he could cast a wider net. If he did well in multiple exams, he would have more options to choose from. This was crucial, especially in a competitive environment where even one bad day could make or break his dreams.

The Safety Net

In a country where millions of students are fighting for a few thousand seats in prestigious colleges, it's only wise to have a backup plan. Think of it like insurance—just as you wouldn't drive without car insurance or live without health insurance, you shouldn't gamble your future on a single entrance exam.

Let's consider Vijay's example. If he was only focusing on the CLAT and it didn't go as planned, his dream of becoming a lawyer could be dashed in an instant. But by also preparing for the SLAT, AILET, and other law entrance exams, he ensured that even if one exam didn't pan out, he had other avenues to explore.

This "safety net" strategy applies to other fields as well. Post graduate management aspirants who only take the CAT might be limiting themselves. By appearing for other exams like XAT, SNAP, or MAT, they increase their chances of securing a seat in top-tier B-schools. In the field of liberal studies, having multiple options opens doors to a wider variety of universities and courses, especially if the student's first choice doesn't come through.

Exposure to Different Formats and Question Types

One of the most underrated benefits of appearing in multiple entrance exams is the exposure to different formats and question types. The CLAT, for example, is quite different from the SLAT in terms of question structure and difficulty level. CLAT focuses heavily on passage based legal reasoning, logical reasoning, and general knowledge, whereas the SLAT places a greater emphasis on quick reading and analytical reasoning. If Vijay only focused on CLAT, he would have missed out on the chance to hone skills relevant to other types of exams.

Similarly, management entrance exams like CAT, XAT, and SNAP each have their unique style of testing. CAT focuses on quantitative ability, logical reasoning, and verbal ability, while XAT includes sections on decision-making and general knowledge. MAT, on the other hand, has more emphasis on data analysis and business-related questions. By preparing for more than one exam, Vijay not only improved his chances but also developed a broader skill set, making him a more well-rounded candidate for various institutions.

Increased Chances of Admission

Let's face it—entrance exams are competitive. The number of seats in top colleges for law, management, and liberal studies is limited, and the competition is fierce. Even the brightest students may miss out on their dream college due to the sheer volume of applicants and the unpredictable nature of cutoffs.

By appearing for multiple exams, students can increase their chances of getting admitted to a top college. Think of it as applying for multiple job positions—if one doesn't work out, you still have others lined up. Vijay, for example, could have applied to a variety of law colleges, each with its own entrance exam, thereby increasing his chances of being accepted. Similarly, for post-graduation, if he did well in multiple management entrance exams, he could choose from a wider pool of institutions.

Preparing for Multiple Exams—An Advantageous Challenge

Some students might argue that preparing for more than one entrance exam is an overwhelming task. It's true that the syllabus for law, management, and liberal studies exams can be extensive, and preparing for multiple exams requires time and effort. But Vijay learned an important lesson along the way: preparation for one exam often overlaps with others. The skills and knowledge needed for CLAT, for instance, were not entirely different from those required for SLAT or AILET. Similarly, many of the subjects in management exams—quantitative ability, reasoning, and general knowledge—are common across most entrance tests.

This overlap made it easier for Vijay to juggle multiple exams. Instead of focusing on one exam exclusively, he divided his preparation in a way that allowed him to cover topics that were common across all exams. And this approach not only saved time but also sharpened his abilities, allowing him to perform better in each test.

The Reality of College Admission Systems

It's important to recognize that college admissions systems, especially for fields like law, management, and liberal studies, are not monolithic. Different colleges have different selection processes, and these processes may change year after year. Some institutions may rely solely on entrance exams, while others may give weightage to board exam marks, extracurricular activities, and interviews. By appearing for more than one entrance exam, students like Vijay are not only casting a wider net but also preparing for different admission criteria.

Moreover, some exams have the added advantage of being conducted by private institutions, offering flexibility in terms of deadlines and application windows. If Vijay had only focused on exams like CLAT and AILET, he could have missed out on lucrative opportunities at private universities that conduct their own entrance exams.

The Psychological Advantage

There is also a psychological advantage to appearing for multiple exams. Students like Vijay, who have multiple exams lined up, tend to feel less anxious about their future. The pressure to perform well in a single exam can be overwhelming, and the fear of failure can cloud judgment and hinder performance. But when you know that you have several opportunities to prove yourself, the mental pressure is significantly reduced.

Appearing for multiple exams gives students a sense of security, knowing that even if one exam doesn't go as planned, they still have others to fall back on. This mental freedom can lead to better performance, as students are not bogged down by the fear of failure in a single exam.

Conclusion

Vijay's journey through the maze of entrance exams was a testament to the importance of planning ahead and being strategic. By appearing for multiple exams, he increased his chances of getting into a top law college, diversified his options, and improved his skill set. What started as a nervous step into the world of competitive exams soon became a calculated move that worked in his favour.

For students in standard 12 preparing for college entrance exams, the message is clear: don't put all your eggs in one basket. By preparing for multiple exams, you not only increase your chances of admission but also expose yourself to diverse opportunities. Whether you're pursuing law, management, liberal studies, or any other field, taking the leap and appearing for more than one entrance exam is a wise strategy—one that ensures you cast a wider net and maximize your chances of success.

After all, when it comes to college admissions, the more opportunities you create for yourself, the better your chances of landing the perfect future.

THE IMPORTANCE OF REVISION FOR ENTRANCE EXAMS: A GUIDE FOR INDIAN STUDENTS IN STD 12

As the clock ticks down toward the day of the entrance exam, the pressure mounts. Whether you're preparing for JEE, NEET, CLAT, or any other entrance exam, the battle is on, and every moment counts. For students in Class 12 in India, the months leading up to the entrance exams are often filled with endless hours of studying, mock tests, and problem-solving. But in all this frantic rush to cover the syllabus, there is one crucial component that too many students overlook: **revision**.

Revision is the unsung hero of exam preparation. It's the phase where you take all the material you've learned, solidify it in your mind, and iron out any creases that might trip you up on exam day. Yet, for many students in India, revision tends to be pushed aside in the quest to tackle "new" content, especially with the overwhelming pressure to perform well in entrance exams for coveted courses like engineering, medicine, law, and business management.

So, why is revision so important for entrance exam success? How can you approach it effectively? And, most importantly, how can revision be the key to cracking those competitive exams that seem like a mountain to climb? Let's break it down.

The Power of Revision: Revisiting the Fundamentals

Revision isn't just about going through your notes or textbooks in a cursory manner; it's about reinforcing and refining the knowledge you've gained throughout the year. It's like polishing a diamond—no matter how bright the stone is, it needs the final touch to make it shine. And that's exactly what revision does for your exam preparation.

1. **Reinforces Memory**

   Let's face it: the sheer amount of information that needs to be crammed into your brain for entrance exams can be overwhelming. You're not just studying for your school board exams; you're also preparing for one or more entrance exams in subjects like physics, chemistry, biology, mathematics, and even logic, economics, or English. The content can be massive. And, the more you study, the more likely you are to forget certain details as time passes. This is where revision becomes invaluable.

   When you revise, you are essentially helping your brain "retain" the information. Revisiting concepts strengthens your memory and ensures that the knowledge stays lodged in your long-term memory. It's like sharpening a knife repeatedly before using it—you make sure it's as effective as possible when the time comes.

2. **Builds Confidence**

   When students prepare for exams, they often go through a cycle of doubt. Even if they've studied hard, they can start to feel unsure about whether they've covered everything or whether they've understood the concepts correctly. Revision is a great way to build confidence.

When you go through your notes, work on practice papers, and solve problems you've already studied, you begin to realize just how much you actually know. The sense of familiarity with the topics builds your confidence and reduces exam-related anxiety. In fact, many students who are underprepared in other areas may still score well if they've done proper revision—because they've already solidified their understanding of the concepts, they're most likely to face.

3. Helps Identify Weaknesses

No matter how prepared you feel, there will always be areas that need a little more attention. Revision provides the perfect opportunity to pinpoint those weak spots. You may realize that certain topics or types of problems consistently trip you up, or you may notice areas where your understanding isn't as solid as it should be.

Once you identify your weaknesses during revision, you can allocate time to focus on them specifically, whether by referring to notes, seeking help from teachers, or watching online tutorials. Revision allows you to tailor your preparation according to your needs, helping you to zero in on the areas that matter most for your success.

The Smart Approach to Revision

While revision is undoubtedly crucial, it's not just about cramming information right before the exam. A hasty, last-minute revision is as ineffective as running a race without training. Effective revision involves planning, strategy, and a well-thought-out approach to maximize your output.

1. **Start Early—Don't Wait for the Last Minute**

   In an ideal world, revision wouldn't just be reserved for the final few weeks before the exam. Waiting until the last minute to revise is like waiting until the final stretch of a marathon to start running—it's too little, too late. To really benefit from revision, you need to start early—at least a month or two before the exam.

   By starting early, you give yourself plenty of time to go over everything at a comfortable pace. You can break down topics into smaller, digestible chunks, ensuring that you cover all of them without feeling rushed. Early revision also helps you identify and address weak spots far in advance, allowing for a more thorough and relaxed approach in the lead-up to exam day.

2. **Break Your Revision into Focused Blocks**

   Attempting to cover everything in one sitting is not only tiring but counterproductive. Instead, break your revision sessions into smaller blocks of time. For instance, work on one subject for 45 minutes to an hour, and then take a short break to recharge. Studies have shown that this method—known as the Pomodoro Technique—helps improve focus and retention.

Additionally, within each block, focus on a specific topic or concept. Don't try to revise an entire chapter in one go. For example, if you're preparing for JEE, devote one session to revising mechanics, another to thermodynamics, and so on. Spacing out your revision will help prevent burnout and keep your mind fresh.

3. **Use Active Recall and Spaced Repetition**

When revising, it's important not to simply read through your notes passively. Instead, use active recall techniques. Close your books, and try to remember key points or solve problems without looking at your notes. This technique strengthens your memory and forces your brain to actively retrieve information.

Along with active recall, incorporate spaced repetition into your revision schedule. This method involves revisiting the same material multiple times at increasing intervals. For instance, you could revise a concept on the first day, again after two days, and then once more after a week. Spaced repetition helps solidify information in your long-term memory and is a highly effective technique for retaining complex concepts and formulas.

4. **Prioritize Important Topics**

In your revision, prioritize important topics that are frequently tested in the entrance exams. Entrance exams often have certain sections or types of questions that tend to appear year after year. By reviewing previous years' question papers and identifying patterns, you can focus your revision on these high-yield topics.

For example, if you're preparing for NEET, you know that biology, especially topics like human physiology and genetics, is crucial. Similarly, for JEE, subjects like calculus and organic chemistry demand your attention. By focusing on high-yield topics, you're maximizing your chances of scoring well while ensuring that you don't waste time on low-yield or less important areas.

5. **Take Mock Tests and Analyse Your Performance**

Mock tests are a cornerstone of any good revision strategy. They simulate the actual exam environment, helping you familiarize yourself with the format, time constraints, and the pressure of a real exam. Moreover, mock tests highlight your strengths and weaknesses, allowing you to adjust your revision strategy accordingly.

Make sure to not just take mock tests but also analyse your performance thoroughly. Look at the types of questions you got wrong and understand why you made those mistakes. Are they due to a lack of knowledge, poor time management, or careless errors? Identifying the reasons behind your mistakes will allow you to avoid repeating them on exam day.

Revision vs. Overworking: Knowing Your Limits

While revision is important, overdoing it can lead to burnout. Many students make the mistake of overworking themselves during the revision phase, thinking that more study equals more success. In reality, overworking can cause stress, fatigue, and mental exhaustion, which negatively affects your performance.

It's essential to know your limits and balance study with adequate breaks and rest. Giving your mind time to relax helps consolidate the information you've studied and refreshes you for the next session.

Final Thoughts: A Key to Success

In the whirlwind of preparing for entrance exams in Class 12, it's easy to get caught up in the race to cover everything. But in the final stages of your preparation, revision is what truly matters. It's your opportunity to consolidate knowledge, fine-tune your understanding, and ensure that the information you've learned is ready to be unleashed on exam day.

For Indian students facing multiple exams with different syllabi, revision isn't just important—it's a game-changer. With the right strategy, a focused approach, and a calm mind, revision can be the difference between a good performance and an outstanding one. Remember, it's not just about working hard; it's about working smart. So, take the time to revise effectively, and you'll walk into that exam hall ready to tackle anything that comes your way.

Balancing Board Exams and Entrance Exam Preparation: A Guide for Std 12 Students in India

For a student in India, Standard 12 is a pivotal year. It's the culmination of years of hard work, the gateway to future careers, and the testing ground for their academic abilities. In this crucial year, students often face the daunting task of preparing for not just their board exams but also for entrance exams that determine their admission to prestigious colleges. Whether it's engineering, medical, law, or business management, the pressure to excel in both is immense. Balancing the preparation for board exams and entrance exams can seem like walking a tightrope, but with the right strategy and mindset, it's not only possible but also rewarding.

The Dilemma: Board Exams vs Entrance Exams

Let's face it: the struggle to balance board exams and entrance exams is as old as the hills in India. Each year, millions of students find themselves in the same boat: juggling school assignments, preparing for exams that determine their college admissions, and fighting off stress along the way. It's a race against time, and many students end up in a frenzy trying to meet deadlines for both school and entrance exam preparation. But here's the rub: one can't afford to compromise on either front. The board exams, which are conducted by various state boards and national boards like CBSE, are crucial for obtaining a passing certificate and securing a seat in universities. On the other hand, entrance exams like JEE, NEET, CLAT, and IPMAT, serve as the gateway to coveted career paths like engineering, medicine, law, and business.

The Pressure Cooker Environment

The pressure on a student in Standard 12 is almost palpable. The stakes are high — one wrong step could lead to disappointment. "I'll make it!" they tell themselves, but the overwhelming weight of the expectations can make the goal feel unattainable. Parents, relatives, and even friends are all watching, waiting for the magic to unfold. The future, for many students, seems to hinge on these two sets of exams.

The problem, however, is that each exam has its own syllabus, format, and level of difficulty. For example, JEE or NEET is known for its highly competitive nature, focusing on subjects like Physics, Chemistry, and Mathematics or Biology. The board exams, on the other hand, require an understanding of a wider range of topics, including subjects that may not be as important for entrance exams but still carry weight in academic grading.

For students preparing for multiple exams, this leads to confusion: Should they focus more on the entrance exams, which have the potential to secure them a place in a prestigious college, or should they prioritize board exams, which affect their overall academic standing? Many students spend sleepless nights thinking about this dilemma. But let's be clear: the solution lies not in choosing one over the other but in managing both effectively.

The Time Crunch: Finding Time for Both

Time, or rather the lack of it, is the most significant challenge faced by students in Standard 12. Between school hours, tuition classes, self-study, and mock exams, it can feel like there are never enough hours in the day. The standard 24 hours suddenly seem too short to accommodate everything that needs to be done. It is easy to become overwhelmed.

However, with effective time management, it is possible to strike a balance. The key is to break down the day into manageable chunks of time and ensure that both board exam preparation and entrance exam preparation are given sufficient attention. This is where time-blocking comes in.

Time-Blocking: The Key to Balancing Both Syllabi

Time-blocking is a strategy that involves scheduling specific blocks of time for different tasks. Instead of trying to multitask or focus on too many things at once, you dedicate a set period to a specific activity. For instance, you can allocate the first two hours of the day to board exam subjects like English or History and the next two hours to subjects like Current Affairs or Logical Reasoning for entrance exam preparation. This strategy ensures that both sets of exams are given due focus.

The evening can be reserved for revision, practice tests, or reviewing difficult concepts. This way, you ensure that both your board exam and entrance exam preparation are evenly distributed throughout the day. It's also crucial to take short breaks in between to avoid burnout.

Creating a Balanced Study Plan

A well-organized study plan is the backbone of successful preparation. A good study plan not only sets goals but also maps out the strategy for how to achieve those goals. Students should start by identifying the topics that overlap between the board exam syllabus and the entrance exam syllabus. For example, in subjects like Physics, the board exam will likely focus on concepts such as mechanics and electricity, which also appear in the entrance exam syllabus. By recognizing these overlaps, students can prepare efficiently for both sets of exams simultaneously.

It's also important to factor in the revision period. As the exams approach, the focus should shift from learning new material to revising and strengthening existing knowledge. This is especially critical for entrance exams, where mock tests and past papers play an essential role in familiarizing students with the format and types of questions.

The Role of Mock Tests: Practice Makes Perfect

Mock tests are an indispensable tool in entrance exam preparation. These tests simulate the actual exam environment, giving students a taste of what to expect on the big day. The idea is to practice under exam-like conditions to build confidence and improve time management skills.

In the case of board exams, mock tests are equally important. They help students familiarize themselves with the format of the board exam, test their knowledge, and improve their writing skills. With entrance exams becoming more competitive by the day, practice in the form of mock tests has become a necessity, not a luxury. Many students have found that taking regular mock tests for both entrance exams and board exams improves their performance significantly.

Mock tests also serve as a reality check. They highlight areas where students need to improve and provide insight into how well they have understood the topics. Students can then tweak their study plans accordingly, focusing on their weak areas while still maintaining a steady pace with the rest of the syllabus.

The Role of School, Coaching, and Self-Study

Students in Standard 12 are not alone in their journey. They have the support of schools, coaching classes, and self-study. A school provides the foundation for board exam preparation, while coaching centers focus more on entrance exam preparation. While both are essential, it's important to strike a balance.

Coaching classes can help students learn specific strategies for cracking entrance exams. Teachers in these classes often offer insights that are tailored to the entrance exam's unique pattern. On the flip side, school teachers focus on broad academic development and also play an essential role in board exam preparation.

That being said, too much reliance on coaching classes or school alone may hinder a student's ability to effectively prepare. Self-study is an integral part of the preparation process. It's where students solidify their understanding, solve practice questions, and reinforce what they've learned in class. For students juggling both exams, dedicating a few hours a day to self-study can provide the much-needed edge.

The Importance of Mental Health: Staying Calm Amid the Storm

As important as academic preparation is, mental health is even more crucial. A student can prepare for hours every day, but if their mental well-being is compromised, it can all go down the drain. Balancing board exams and entrance exams can be mentally taxing, and it's essential to take care of one's mental health.

To keep stress levels in check, students should ensure they are getting enough sleep, eating well, and exercising regularly. Yoga and meditation are also known to help reduce stress. Students should also take breaks from their studies to relax and engage in activities they enjoy.

It's also important to develop a positive mindset. Instead of focusing on the overwhelming nature of the task at hand, students should focus on taking it one day at a time. Breaking down the task into smaller, manageable steps can make it seem less daunting. Students should remind themselves that they are capable of handling both sets of exams, and with the right approach, they can emerge victorious.

Parents: The Pillars of Support

Parents have a significant role to play in a student's academic journey, especially during the intense preparation period for board exams and entrance exams. However, it's essential for parents to be supportive without being overbearing. The pressure to perform can be immense, and parents need to understand that their child needs both encouragement and space.

Parents should create a conducive environment for study, free from distractions. They can also help by ensuring that their child is maintaining a balanced lifestyle, with adequate time for rest, play, and relaxation. Instead of pressuring their children, parents should be there as emotional support, offering reassurance when things seem tough.

Conclusion: The Path to Success

Balancing board exams and entrance exam preparation is undoubtedly a tough task for students in Standard 12. The key to managing this balancing act lies in a well-structured study plan, effective time management, and a strong support system. By recognizing the overlaps between the two syllabi, practicing regularly through mock tests, and maintaining good mental health, students can manage both successfully.

While it may seem like an uphill climb, it's important to remember that with persistence, focus, and the right strategy, achieving success in both exams is not just a dream, but a tangible reality. Students should remind themselves that this period, though challenging, will eventually pass, and the reward will be worth the effort. Balancing board exams and entrance exams is all about smart work, not just hard work. It's about learning to navigate the chaos with grace and determination.

The Perils of Last-Minute Preparation for College Entrance Exams: A Cautionary Tale for Indian Students

It was the middle of January when Sudarshan realized that his entrance exam for admission to the most prestigious engineering colleges in India was just a few weeks away. The countdown had begun, and panic started to creep in as the reality of his situation hit him like a ton of bricks. Sudarshan had spent the entire year in a relaxed mode, believing that there was plenty of time to catch up later. But now, with the clock ticking faster than ever, the thought of preparing at the last minute seemed like the only option left.

"I'll manage," he muttered to himself, as he flipped through the pages of his Physics book, his eyes barely scanning the content. But the more he read, the more overwhelmed he felt. The vast syllabus, the complex formulas, and the sheer amount of information to memorize seemed insurmountable. He had procrastinated for so long that now, all he could do was cram — and cram hard. But deep down, he knew this was a dangerous game.

Sudarshan's story is one that many students across India can relate to, especially those preparing for college entrance exams like the JEE (Joint Entrance Examination), NEET (National Eligibility cum Entrance Test), CLAT (Common Law Admission Test), or other state-level exams. These exams, which are often a make-or-break point in a student's academic career, require months, if not years, of preparation. However, as the exam date looms closer, some students find themselves relying on the unwise strategy of last-minute cramming. But why is it bad to prepare at the last minute for exams, particularly in the context of Indian students? Let's delve into the reasons.

The Myth of the "Cramming Success"

The first issue with last-minute preparation is the misconception that cramming can yield success. It's a belief many students cling to, especially during the pressure-packed final days before exams. "I've done this before; I'll be fine," they think. The reality, however, is much harsher. Cramming doesn't allow students to truly understand the material; it merely helps them memorize it in the short term. The night before the exam, Sudarshan might have been able to memorize a few formulas, but his understanding of the concepts remained shallow. The pressure of trying to stuff a mountain of information into his head in a short period is simply not sustainable.

Studies show that last-minute cramming is less effective in the long term because it hampers the brain's ability to process and retain information. The human brain absorbs and retains information better through gradual learning and consistent revision, which cramming simply cannot achieve. The stress and anxiety of last-minute preparation can actually impair cognitive functions, making it even harder to recall what you've studied during the exam.

In Sudarshan's case, the cramming marathon led to exhaustion and frustration. By the time the exam came around, he was sleep-deprived and mentally drained, which affected his performance. This is a scenario that countless students experience every year, but it doesn't have to be this way.

The Dangers of Procrastination

One of the primary reasons why students resort to last-minute preparation is procrastination — putting off until tomorrow what can be done today. Sudarshan had fallen victim to this trap, thinking that there would always be more time. This mindset is incredibly common among students, especially when the syllabus seems overwhelming or when the student is unsure of where to start. The procrastination monster whispers, "You'll have time later," but that "later" never seems to come.

Procrastination is like a snowball rolling down a hill, gaining momentum as time goes by. Initially, it feels like there's no rush, but soon the task becomes insurmountable, and panic sets in. This is exactly what happens when students leave their preparation until the last minute. As the exam date nears, the feeling of being unprepared intensifies, causing stress and anxiety that further hinder the ability to focus.

The reality is that Indian entrance exams are some of the most competitive and challenging exams in the world. Parental, Peer and Social pressures don't help either. The pressure to perform well is immense, and procrastination only exacerbates that pressure. By leaving preparation to the last minute, students risk not only their academic future but also their mental well-being. A student who has procrastinated might find themselves staring at a textbook in desperation, but their mind is too frazzled to absorb any meaningful information. The result is a vicious cycle of stress, procrastination, and poor performance.

Inadequate Understanding of Concepts

Another key issue with last-minute preparation is the lack of conceptual understanding. When Sudarshan hurriedly flipped through the chapters, he was focusing on memorizing formulas and facts rather than understanding the underlying concepts. In entrance exams like the JEE and NEET, merely memorizing information is not enough. The exams are designed to test not just rote knowledge but also a deep understanding of the subject matter and the ability to apply concepts in various scenarios.

For example, in the JEE, Physics and Mathematics require students to solve complex problems that involve multiple concepts. If a student hasn't grasped the fundamentals properly, they won't be able to solve these problems efficiently. This is where Sudarshan fell short. By cramming at the last minute, he missed the chance to truly understand the material and build a strong foundation.

Moreover, when students rely solely on last-minute preparation, they often skip over critical topics that require more time and attention. Sudarshan, like many others, may have focused on areas he felt more comfortable with, neglecting the challenging topics that would ultimately decide his fate in the exam. The syllabus for Indian entrance exams is vast, and rushing through it leaves no room for a thorough understanding.

The Importance of Consistency and Revision

The key to success in any competitive exam, especially in India, lies in consistent and structured preparation. The earlier a student starts, the better equipped they are to understand the material in depth, identify weak areas, and revise thoroughly before the exam. This kind of preparation not only boosts confidence but also helps reduce exam-related anxiety.

Take Sudarshan's situation as an example. Had he started his preparation months in advance, he would have had the time to break down his study sessions into manageable chunks. This would have allowed him to focus on one concept at a time, practice problems regularly, and revise key topics. Consistent revision is vital because it helps reinforce the material, making it easier to recall during the exam.

When students prepare early and stick to a routine, they experience less stress and perform better. It's a simple equation: hard work over time equals results. It's like the tortoise and the hare story — slow and steady wins the race. A student who prepares consistently, gradually building their knowledge, is far more likely to succeed than one who crams in the final days.

Health and Well-being

One of the most overlooked consequences of last-minute preparation is its impact on a student's physical and mental health. Sudarshan, like many other students, pulled all-nighters, drank excessive amounts of coffee, and barely slept in the days leading up to the exam. This approach, though seemingly productive in the short term, took a heavy toll on his well-being. The lack of sleep and the high levels of stress made him feel drained, both physically and mentally.

Sleep deprivation, poor diet, and constant anxiety lead to a weakened immune system, making students more susceptible to illness. Moreover, the mental toll of cramming can lead to burnout, leaving students unable to perform at their best when the exam finally arrives.

Last-minute cramming often causes students to neglect their health, which can have long-term effects. A good night's sleep, regular exercise, and a balanced diet are crucial for maintaining focus and clarity of thought. By preparing in advance, students can avoid the chaos of last-minute studying and take better care of their health.

The Social and Emotional Toll

Beyond the academic and physical aspects, last-minute preparation also takes an emotional toll on students. As Sudarshan sat alone in his room, flipping through his notes, the weight of expectations — his own and his parents' — pressed heavily on him. In India, where entrance exams are often seen as the gateway to a successful career, the pressure to perform is immense. Students who cram at the last minute often feel isolated and anxious, unsure of whether their efforts will be enough.

The emotional stress of last-minute preparation can lead to anxiety, depression, and even self-doubt. Students who have procrastinated might find themselves comparing their progress with that of their peers, which only amplifies feelings of inadequacy. This vicious cycle of stress and comparison can seriously affect a student's mental health, leading to a decline in self-esteem and confidence.

As Sudarshan walked out of the exam hall, he couldn't shake the feeling that he had fallen short. He had given it his best shot, but deep down, he knew that last-minute preparation had cost him the chance to truly excel. While it's true that some students might manage to scrape through with last-minute cramming, the risks far outweigh the rewards. Last-minute preparation for college entrance exams is a high-risk strategy that undermines a student's potential, their health, and their future prospects.

In the end, the key to success lies in consistent, methodical, and well-paced preparation. Indian students must learn to take a proactive approach to their studies, managing their time wisely and avoiding the temptation to procrastinate. Success isn't just about cramming at the last minute; it's about smart, steady effort over time. After all, Rome wasn't built in a day, and neither is exam success. By preparing early, students can enter their exams with confidence, knowing they have given their best — not just in the final days, but throughout their journey.

PART 3: TIME MANAGEMENT

Effective Time Management for Indian Students Preparing for Both School Board Exams and College Entrance Exams

For Indian students in Class 12, the pressure can be overwhelming. The final year of school is a time filled with expectations, aspirations, and, yes, a fair amount of stress. Students are expected to focus on the school board exams, which are crucial for their academic records and future prospects, while simultaneously preparing for college entrance exams that can determine their next academic steps. The balancing act of managing both these goals often feels like walking a tightrope.

The juggling act between board exams and entrance exam preparation demands excellent time management skills. Without a structured approach, it is easy to get overwhelmed by the sheer volume of syllabus and the constant pressure to perform. For many students, the question becomes: "How do I effectively manage my time so that I do justice to both?"

This essay will explore the concept of effective time management for students in Class 12, focusing on strategies, tools, and practical tips to help students manage their preparation for both school board exams and college entrance exams. By the end of this piece, readers will be equipped with the knowledge to plan their time wisely and perform efficiently under pressure.

The Double Whammy: Navigating Board Exams and Entrance Exams

In India, Class 12 marks the pinnacle of a student's academic career. School board exams and entrance exams for various colleges are often seen as two separate beasts, but they are undeniably interconnected. School board exams typically focus on assessing a student's understanding of subjects they have been learning over the last two years, while entrance exams, such as those for engineering (JEE), medicine (NEET), law (CLAT), or business management (IPMAT), require a more focused approach on specific subjects or aptitude.

For students, the dilemma arises from the fact that these exams are scheduled close to each other, demanding a high level of preparation in parallel. Balancing preparation for both can often feel like trying to catch a dozen spinning plates at once. But the trick lies in effective time management.

Why Time Management is Crucial for Class 12 Students

Time management is more than just about making a schedule or keeping a to-do list. It's about strategically allocating your time so that you work smarter, not harder. With the pressure of preparing for both school board exams and entrance exams, poor time management can lead to burnout, frustration, and a subpar performance.

Here are a few reasons why time management is paramount for Class 12 students:

1. **Limited Time and High Expectations**: Between school assignments, revision, and entrance exam preparation, students are pressed for time. A lack of proper time management could lead to insufficient preparation for one or both exams.

2. **Stress and Overwhelm**: When students don't plan their time effectively, they risk feeling overwhelmed. Anxiety about exams and the looming deadlines can become mentally taxing, affecting performance.

3. **Maximizing Productivity**: With the right time management techniques, students can avoid procrastination, stay on top of their study materials, and boost their productivity. This is the key to excelling in both school and entrance exams.

4. **Avoiding Last-Minute Cramming**: Proper time management helps students avoid the trap of last-minute cramming, a habit that not only increases stress but also hampers long-term retention of knowledge.

Steps to Effective Time Management

Now that we understand the importance of time management, let's take a deeper look at the specific strategies that can help Class 12 students efficiently manage their time while preparing for both school board exams and entrance exams.

1. **Set Clear Goals and Priorities**

   The first step in time management is setting clear and realistic goals. Students need to know exactly what they are working towards — whether it is mastering a particular chapter in physics, revising for the chemistry exam, or solving mock tests for JEE or NEET. Without clear goals, it becomes difficult to measure progress and stay on track.

   It's crucial to break down long-term goals into smaller, more manageable targets. For instance, instead of saying, "I need to study for my board exams," break it down into specific goals like "Complete Chapter 1 of Chemistry today," or "Solve 20 math problems from the JEE syllabus today."

   Also, prioritize your goals. Some subjects will require more time and effort than others, and that's okay. For example, a student preparing for the JEE may prioritize subjects like Physics and Mathematics, while a student aiming for NEET may devote more time to Biology. Identifying your priorities will help you allocate your time effectively.

2. **Create a Timetable**

   A timetable is one of the most effective tools for managing time. It acts as a road map that helps students navigate their daily schedule, ensuring they make time for everything — school, revision, practice, and rest.

   Start by creating a daily or weekly timetable that includes time slots for school, self-study, and entrance exam preparation. Be realistic about how much time you can devote to each subject. For instance, mornings could be reserved for school subjects, while evenings could be dedicated to entrance exam preparation.

An effective timetable should also include adequate breaks to refresh the mind. Studying for hours without a break is counterproductive and can lead to burnout. Short 10–15-minute breaks between study sessions help maintain focus and productivity.

3. **Study Smart, Not Hard**

For Class 12 students preparing for both school and entrance exams, studying smarter is key to effective time management. Students should focus on understanding concepts rather than rote memorization, especially for subjects that require problem-solving, such as mathematics and physics. Concepts are the foundation, and once they're clear, solving problems becomes much easier.

One smart approach is to integrate the preparation for both exams. For example, the physics syllabus for both the school board exam and JEE is similar, so revising the same chapter for both exams at the same time makes sense. Similarly, subjects like Chemistry or Biology for NEET and Class 12 can be tackled simultaneously.

A student can also solve mock tests or previous years' question papers for both school exams and entrance exams. This not only helps in better time management but also in identifying weak areas early on.

4. **Use the Pomodoro Technique**

One of the most effective time management techniques is the Pomodoro Technique. This method involves studying for 25 minutes, followed by a 5-minute break. After completing four "Pomodoros," take a longer 15–30-minute break. The idea behind this technique is to maintain focus and productivity while preventing mental fatigue.

For students in Class 12, this method works wonders because it helps break down the long hours of study into manageable chunks. It's especially helpful for tackling difficult or time-consuming subjects that require intense concentration.

5. **Minimize Distractions**

In today's age, distractions are everywhere. Social media, mobile phones, and the constant lure of entertainment can easily derail a study session. Therefore, it's important to create an environment conducive to studying.

Set up a designated study area that is free from distractions. Put your phone on silent or, better yet, in another room while studying. Inform your family members about your study hours so they don't disturb you. The key is to minimize distractions so that the time you do spend studying is focused and productive.

6. **Track Your Progress**

Regularly tracking your progress is crucial for staying on track. Set weekly or monthly checkpoints to evaluate how well you are adhering to your timetable and goals. Ask yourself questions like, "Have I completed all the chapters I planned to revise?" or "How many mock tests have I taken for my entrance exam?"

Tracking progress will help identify areas where you may need to devote more time. If you find that you are falling behind on your entrance exam preparation or haven't completed a specific school subject, it's time to reassess and adjust your timetable accordingly.

7. **Stay Healthy**

Good time management isn't just about managing study hours — it's also about managing your physical and mental health. A healthy body and mind are essential for effective studying.

Get sufficient sleep, eat a balanced diet, and make time for exercise or outdoor activities. When students are healthy, they are better able to concentrate, retain information, and handle stress. Additionally, mindfulness techniques such as meditation can help reduce anxiety and improve focus.

8. **Don't Overburden Yourself**

It's easy to fall into the trap of overloading your timetable with an unrealistic number of tasks, thinking that this will increase productivity. However, this often leads to burnout. Avoid trying to do everything at once. Instead, focus on what's important and give yourself enough time to understand the material.

If you feel overwhelmed, it's okay to take a step back and reassess. Time management is about balance, not about cramming every minute with studying. Taking regular breaks, pursuing hobbies, or simply relaxing is necessary to maintain overall well-being.

Conclusion

Time management is an art, one that requires practice, self-awareness, and dedication. For Class 12 students preparing for both school board exams and entrance exams, it is essential to have a clear strategy to balance their time effectively. By setting clear goals, creating a timetable, studying smartly, using techniques like Pomodoro, minimizing distractions, and staying healthy, students can successfully navigate the demands of both school and entrance exam preparation.

It's a tough road, but with the right approach, it's definitely manageable. Remember, time is a limited resource, and managing it effectively can make all the difference in achieving success — both in school and in college entrance exams. And as the saying goes, "Well begun is half done." The sooner you start planning, the sooner you'll see the rewards of your hard work.

How to Get More than 24 Hours in a Day?

I don't have enough time!

I am so busy; I can't do everything that I want!

One of the most common complaints that I get from students (and many an adult as well!), is the lack of time.

24 hours don't seem to be enough for handling all work that seem to keep piling up.

Keep in mind, I am a teacher who works with students of grades 11 and 12, for most of my day. What with hours of school and tuition classes, there barely seems to be enough time available for students, to do other activities. Once the student comes to grade 10 (the all-dreaded BOARD YEAR!), it is common to see them being forced to sacrifice a lot of their loved extracurricular activities and hobbies, in order to study. This gets worse in grades 11 and 12. Dark circles and grumpy moods seem common in students who try to do well in academics.

And yet, there are those who seem to be participating all sort of extracurricular activities like sports, quiz competitions, Model United Nations, etc. without compromising on their academics.

How does one manage to do all that and more?

Well, if you have some time to read my *gyaan* on this issue, then proceed further.

Warning: I am going to brag a lot in the coming passages.

Here's a snapshot of what my schedules have looked like during my school and college days. If you think, I have managed to do a lot of things that you wish you had time for, then this would probably help.

During my school days, I had the aura of being a studious child. Even today, when I meet some of my old school mates (who were mere acquaintances, and not very close to me), the general impression that they seem to have had about me, was that *"Sathya was a very studious person. He was the school topper."* However, not many people seem to know much about my life outside school. The perception was that I devoted almost all my waking hours to the pursuit of good grades.

Well, nothing could be farther from the truth. While I did manage to get excellent grades in almost all school tests, I was not a typical bookworm, who spent hours mugging textbooks and notes.

I am not a very physical person. My mother perpetually complains about my lack of interest in sports at present. However, during my childhood, she was the one who got me enrolled for swimming classes. For over seven years, I was a regular swimmer. While I never swam competitively, it was a regular activity that I pursued for almost an hour every day.

I was enrolled for basic Karate and Skating workshops and have learned the basic skills in both areas.

Drawing has always been one of my favourite hobbies. I was enrolled in a drawing and sketching class, run by an old Bengali lady. I have spent countless weekends during my school days, learning the basics of drawing. I have cleared both the elementary and intermediate levels of certification of drawing. I participated and won numerous drawing competitions in the city.

The Bengali lady was member of a Bengali Cultural Organisation, which used to conduct cultural activities during the *Durga Pujo* period. I participated in numerous stage plays (in Bengali) and gave performances in public.

Once, the organisation conducted a simple quiz competition for youngsters. I participated and did well. This gave me quite a kick. I grew more interested in the world of quizzing and started participating in numerous quiz competitions through my school. Thanks to a couple of my school teachers, who encouraged us tremendously, my *Sardarji* partner and I became well known in the local Quizzing circuit!

I am a stage hound. During the annual function at school, I always participated in every performance that my class would put up.

I cannot claim to be a good dancer. Nevertheless, I would religiously show up for all practice sessions (after school hours), and do my best to learn the dance moves and perform them on stage. During my 10th Board year, I was part of my school group that represented our school and city at a district level dramatics competition.

My father loves reading books. Educated in the vernacular medium at school level, when he secured admission in the prestigious Regional College of Engineering (REC – Now NIT Trichy), he realised the importance of English. He picked up the habit of reading English novels, in order to build his proficiency in the language.

During my early childhood days, he used to sit with my sister and I and tell us the plots of the various novels that he would read. This developed a love for reading in both my sister and me. My parents very smartly would reward us with story books for all sort of achievements. The association of story books with rewards, developed a passion for reading, a love that exists till date.

I was always fond of eating variety of foods. My mother encouraged me to try my hand at cooking simple dishes at home. My first attempt at cooking simple Potato cutlets (from a recipe that I read in one my subscribed Kids Magazine) was appreciated by paternal Grandmother, a venerable old lady, who strictly followed orthodox traditions herself, but encouraged everyone else to be as modern as they wished to be. This developed my passion for food and cooking.

When I entered Engineering college, I carried forward my passion for reading and would spend a lot of time in consuming novels. My tradition of participating in all sorts of cultural activities continued. Not only did I sing and act, but also ended up compering a couple of those functions.

At school level, as is common in many Indian schools, my stellar academic record made me a natural choice for being the class monitor.

At college level, I stood for class representative elections in the first year. I did not win. However, that firmly established me in the group as a leader and go-getter. In my third year, I was selected to be the treasurer of the college committee – a post that was created, just so that I could be an official post holder in various committees. In my final year, I voluntarily chose to be the college vice general-secretary. I could have been the general-secretary. However, the final semester of my department was supposed to be entirely devoted to on-site projects. To avoid doing injustice to college affairs, I decided to serve as the vice general-secretary.

Cut to my post graduate college days. In the initial days, when various committees were being formed, I volunteered to be part of the placements team. Through a selection process, I not only got into the placement team, but was also selected to be one of the chief placement coordinators for the department.

I volunteered my web designing and development skills and became the go-to person for designing all sort of posters and creatives for most of the events organised by the department.

In my final year of MBA, I practically managed the department website for our business festival. In addition to my duties as one of the chief placement coordinators, I represented my department at the institute level senate committee. I served as the department ambassador for new students.

Now, with all these activities at school and college level, how did I do in my studies?

I won the best all-rounder award in my undergraduate days and graduate with one of the highest percentages.

I won the best all-rounder award at B-School and graduated with one of the highest CGPAs, (9.2) in my batch.

So, my academics suffered not a bit.

Bragging done…

Gyaan shuru…

Did I do justice to all the roles and responsibilities that I assumed?

Did I have to sacrifice a lot of things, to be able to manage all that stuff?

How did I get enough time to do it all?

The answer to the first question: I did not take on the various roles and responsibilities in order to make an impressive resume. I never sat for college placements at any level. I had already planned to venture out on my own, immediately after my engineering was done. I voluntarily stepped out of the placement process at B-School (a bold, yet surprising decision – considering the fact that I was one of the chief placement coordinators for the batch!). So, building my resume was never on my mind. I did what I did, because I loved doing all those activities. I never did it for any recognition. Although, I must confess to a huge sense of pride, when one of the strictest professors at B-School (the one whose subject was my least favourite), complimented me on being hands on and wearing so many different hats during my tenure on campus.

The answer to the second question: Forget sacrificing things! At times I felt, I had too much spare time on my hands and was wasting it on frivolous stuff! I was introduced to the wonderful, yet time wasting world of movie downloads and binge-watching shows during my time on campus. I remember watching tons of shows (F.R.I.E.N.D.S., House, random movies…) during my free hours.

Which brings us to that all important question: How the **** did I manage to find enough time to do it all?

1. **Be Attentive**: One of the biggest problems that students face, is finding enough time for learning things and revising concepts. If you have paid keen attention in class, taken copious notes and made sure that you have conceptual clarity in what you have just been taught, you actually do not need a lot of time outside the classroom, for learning and revising concepts.

2. **Reading speed**: I must admit, my passion for reading and hours of reading practice, has given me insane speed for reading written material. I can probably read three to four times faster than an average reader. With a clear focus while reading, comprehension of the written text becomes easy. As a result, I take way less time to read and understand text, as compared to an average reader. Who knew, reading a lot of novels would come in handy for revising class notes!

3. **Division of time**: I need to spend two hours every day in reading newspapers. Does that mean, I need to find a continuous slot of two hours? No. I could

read the papers in 8 slots of 15 minutes each, and still claim a total reading time of 2 hours. I would keep my novel on hand wherever I went. Waiting for my food order to be packed at a café? Read a couple of pages. Riding in a cab to reach a mall. Read a couple of pages. Waiting for the lecturer to arrive in class and start the lecture? Read a couple of pages. Finding small slots of 10-15 minutes, throughout the day, is way too easy. Most people tend to spend these time slots doing nothing. Why not catch up on a small part of some important task in the free time that you have?

That, in my not-so-humble opinion, is my secret to time management!

PART 4: MINDSET

On Why Tough is Good

"Sir, your mock tests are so tough! I don't get good scores in any of them. I gave the test from XYZ institute and scored so well in that! Why don't you give me easy mocks?"

I am no psychologist. However, years of experience, tell me that instant gratification is an addictive thing. For a student, good marks on an internal test do not seem to hold any less value than a good result on a main examination. An internal exam is considered to be an end, rather than a mean for achieving something larger.

This has led to a dangerous phenomenon. Students and parents seem to set a lot of store by the scores achieved in internal evaluation tests and model test papers. They get easily disturbed by low scores on these tests.

Let us try to understand the true purpose of any exam. It all starts with education. The purpose of school/college education is to gain knowledge and expertise in certain specific areas.

For example, let us take the case of Mathematics as a subject. At school level, one is expected to get a fundamental education on the basics. Start with numbers. Learn the basic mathematical operators like addition, subtraction, multiplication and division. Understand the basic concepts of ratio and proportion. Understand simple geometrical shapes like triangles. Learn forming and solving equations. Learn what the Pythagorean theorem is.

Are we done with these basic concepts? Good. Now, when you are introduced with the basics of Trigonometry, it will not seem like all Greek and Latin. Sin, Cos, Tan … nothing but the ratios of the lengths of the sides of a right-angled triangle. Does the formular $\sin^2 x + \cos^2 x = 1$ seem intimidating? What if I told you that it is nothing but an application of the Pythagorean theorem, which you know so well?

Does coordinate geometry intimidate you? Do you struggle to remember the distance formula? The distance between the points (x_1, y_1) and (x_2, y_2) on the coordinate plane can be derived using the formula $((x_2 - x_1)^2 + (y_2 - y_1)^2)^{1/2}$. Seems intimidating? What if I told you that this formula can easily be derived by using nothing more than the good old Pythagorean theorem.

Believe me, once you know your basic concepts, it may take a while to correlate them to the advanced rules. But once you have worked out the advanced concepts by applying the basic ones, you will never struggle to retain those advanced concepts in your memory.

As learning concepts is a long process, it is wise to keep evaluating one's progress along the path. If the student has demonstrated a reasonably good grasp of the basics, it is natural to progress to more complex concepts. However, if the student lacks a good grasp over the basics, it would be a great disservice to the student to burden them with more complex concepts.

Here is where, an internal assessment test plays a vital role. A strict evaluation of the student's progress would give a good insight into what the student has actually learned. A poor score on the test in not necessarily an indictment of the student's learning capacity or dedication. It can merely indicate the need to put in more effort in grasping concepts. It can often give the teacher a better insight into the student's ability to learn and a good teacher can often use this as feedback to better tailor their delivery of knowledge, to suit the learning style of the student. Admittedly, it increases the work load of the teacher. However, a good teacher does not worry about the additional hours that need to be put in. What matters, is that the student should emerge at the end of the term with a solid grasp of all that needs to be learned.

Going back to my previous example, if a student has a very good foundation in the topics of ratio proportion, triangles and the Pythagorean theorem, the topic of Trigonometry would take some time to get used too. But once the student works out the relation between the basic concepts and this new subject, it seems easier than they thought it would be. On the other hand, if the basic concepts are not embedded in one's brain, and the student has cleared exams testing the basic concepts on the strength of rote learning and easy evaluation, then "advanced" concepts like Trigonometry and Coordinate Geometry will seem like an overwhelming burden

Sadly, there seems to be apathy all around. While students (and in many cases, their parents) don't seem to care about acquisition of knowledge, but only care about the acquisition of a certificate, the teacher also seems to care more about the number of students who have "passed" rather than the number of students who have actually gained useful knowledge.

The primary school teacher does not worry about the student being well equipped to crack questions on Trigonometry and Coordinate Geometry at high school level. Neither the student nor the parent seems to think in advance about what they would need for the upper grades. As long as the student has got an A+ or 90% and above score on the mark sheet in the lower grade, everyone is happy.

With such sad conditions, the easy way out for all parties concerned, is to create simple assessment test, which any half competent person could score well on. The student is happy for having received high marks. The parent is happy at this "progress" of the child and the teacher does not have to face accusations of not having taught the subject well.

As a result of this, the phenomenon of "teaching the test" has started becoming the norm. Teachers have started identifying the "exact syllabus" of any exam. They make sure that the students are well versed on these limited topics, nothing more nothing less. Students think that a limited syllabus is easy to handle. As long as they are tested from the limited number of topics that they have to study, they are sure to score well. Happiness all around! In case an exam setter commits the sacrilege of asking a question from "out of syllabus", students are up in arms against the exam. A huge hue and cry is raised and the question is demanded to be scrapped from the paper, or compensatory marks are to be awarded to all students.

Is this really what we need education to be? Dumbing down of concepts and standards, just for people to feel good about themselves?

Coming back to my philosophy of not providing easy practice papers to my students…

Consider this: You are a weight lifter. You have been regularly training to lift a weight of up to 100 kilograms. You definitely would find it difficult, if not impossible, on you first attempt. You could probably lift only 25 kilograms. However, with regular practice and proper training, you slowly start increasing your capacity. In a month, you have increased your capacity to about 50 kilograms. With a few months of intense practice, you finally manage to lift 100 kilograms. On the other hand, you competition is training to lift a maximum weight of 75 kilograms. They manage to reach this goal, in about the same time as you reach yours.

Now comes the day of the actual weight lifting competition. The rules of lifting now specify that you need to be able to lift a weight of 80 kilograms in order to win. Your competitor has trained for a maximum weight of 75 kilograms. Will they be able to handle the additional weight of a mere 5 kilograms? On the other hand, your intensive training has empowered you to handle 20 kilograms more than what you actually need on the day that it matters the most. It is almost a certainty that victory will be yours.

It is not for nothing that the old adage says, *"If you sweat in peace, you will not bleed in war."*

My interpretation of this saying is that, when you train for more than what is required, you can handle anything that is thrown at you, on the day that it matters the most.

I tell my students, compared to almost all the actual entrance test papers, my model test papers are all tough as nails. However, when you practice diligently and learn how to maximise your score in my tests, on the day of the exam – you will breeze through the questions like hot knife through butter.

The choice is yours – do you wish to have the illusory satisfaction of doing well in the practice test papers and struggle with a tough one on the day of the actual exam, or do you wish to sweat it out during your preparation time and have a cakewalk on the day that it matters the most?

Remember: Tough is Good

Students are not to be underestimated. After hearing all this gyaan that I spout, I am often presented with this question: "What if the actual exam turns out to be tough?"

Fair enough.

My line "tough is good" still stand true.

Imagine a situation where ten thousand students are sitting for an exam. You are in the exam hall, all ready to crack a paper that (in the words of your truly, should be "easier" than the mock test papers that you have attempted during your preparation period). The question paper land in front of you. You open the test booklet and are faced with a bunch of questions that are tougher than what you dreamed of.

The natural reaction is to panic. You start cursing the entity that set this paper. You start cursing the person who prepared you for this test. You start having nightmares about a poor result. You start panicking about the outcome.

What you should be telling yourself, is this: Wow! The paper is tough! Every student is facing the same set of questions that I am. If it is tough for me, so is it for all the others.

This naturally eliminates my competition to a large extent. Students, who prepared with easy mock papers, are definitely in a soup.

Once the exam answer sheets are evaluated, the overall results will be low. The infamous "cut-off" marks needed to qualify in this exam, are bound to come down. What am I panicking for? I don't need to score a preset number. I just need to perform better than the competition. As long as I keep my cool, and focus on answering all those questions which I know, I am going to get a good outcome on this test.

Let's put this in terms of numbers.

Scenario 1: It's an easy paper. I manage to score 99/100. Wow! Seems like a good result. But what if everyone else manages to get a 100/100 on the test? I am still at the bottom of the pile.

Scenario 2: The paper is extremely tough. I manage to score a paltry 50 marks. However, if the competition is stuck with scores less than 50, I am still ahead of the pack!

Remember, in entrance exams (unlike school board exams, where any student with a score higher than the pass marks, is deemed to have qualified), you are expected to score just more than everyone else.

In conclusion, ***Tough. Is. Good.***

The choice is yours.

How to Face Your Fear of Exams (And Why It's Not as Scary as You Think)

If Public Speaking and Death are the top fears for most people, exams must also be ranked pretty high on the list.

It is not uncommon to see children have a bad tummy ache on certain mornings, when they know that a test is about to be conducted at school. Even adults dread the very thought of facing an exam.

Why do people hate exams?

Fear of failure!

The best way to face fear is to confront it.

Here's a simple exercise that I conduct with any student who comes to me in a panic before an exam.

I ask, *"What is the worst thing that can happen in this exam?"*

Student: *"I will fail in this exam."*

Me: *"Okay. So what?"*

At this point, the student would look at me, as if I have grown a pair of horns and a tail.

Student: *"What do you mean, by so what? I will FAIL!"*

Me: *"Yes. I heard that. So, my question to you is, what happens when you fail in the exam?"*

Student: *"I will not get admission to the college of my choice."*

Me: *"Right. That is true. You do not get admission to the college of your choice. So, what happens next?"*

Student: *"I will have to take a drop year and prepare for the entrance exams again, or I will have to settle for a lesser college."*

Me: *"Right. If you take a drop year and history repeats itself, we are in a loop and will be back to this same point in our conversation. Let us explore the other route. How would you get into a lesser college?"*

Student: *"I will have to take admissions based on the merit of my 12th Board results."*

Me: *"Correct. Now assume that you do not manage to secure admission in any college, as you got very bad results in your board exams."*

At this point, the student is in a visible state of panic. She is aghast at the turn of our conversation.

Me: *"Remember, we are talking about hypothetical situations. So, assume that you failed miserably in your 12th board exams as well. What is the next thing that is going to take place?"*

Student: *"My parents would kill me!"*

Me: *"Seriously? Do you think so less of your parents that they will commit murder for a poor result?"*

Student: *"No. I mean, they will get very angry and ..."*

Me: *"And what…? What do you think will happen?"*

Student: *"Nooooo… I don't want to even think about that situation!!!"*

Me: *"I am forcing you to go down that path. Your parents have just received the information that you have failed miserably in your board exams as well. The initial reaction would be of anger, shock, dismay, disappointment, frustration and what not… But all that will last for a short while. Then what?"*

Student: *"I don't know."*

Me: *"Do you think there are no options left for you?"*

Student: *"Obviously. There is nothing left to do."*

Me: *"I don't know about you. But let me tell you what I think, my parents would do. After the initial hullabaloo about the bad outcome, my father would most probably ask me to set up a Street Food stall or start doing some sort of manual labour and start earning an income. Do you think, people who earn a daily wage through such means cannot achieve success in life?"*

At this point of time, the student would most probably come to the realisation that even in the worst-case scenario, there is always a choice. Maybe, the choices are not the best ones. However, there is always a choice!

One of the biggest fears that we face is that Indian malaise of *"Log kya kahenge?"* (what will others say about us?)

The fear of being poorly thought about, is often in the mind of the person. Students are afraid of being looked down upon by their friends and relatives.

If someone thinks so poorly about you, do you really think they are your true friends and well-wishers? People love to gossip about others. Stupid as it may seem, they love to talk about the misery of others. They seem to take wicked pleasure in talking about the downfall of people, behind their backs. However, how does the gossip affect my future? Why do I care about the impression that some third party has about me? What matters, is what I think about myself? In a realistic scenario, it matters what my parents think about me.

In reality, while parents may be disappointed in the short term, in the long run, they tend to be supportive. They are our well-wishers. In most cases, they are willing to go above and beyond their means to see their child succeed.

Once the student has logically worked out the worst possible outcomes in this scenario, they come to the realisation that things are not as bad as they seem.

Are they really going to perform that badly in the entrance exam? Are they really going to perform that badly in their board exams? Are they really going to be faced with the prospect of getting no admission to any college? Are they really going to be left with no means to earn a livelihood?

The answer to most of these questions is a resounding NO!

When things aren't as dark as you would lead yourself to believe, then what are you worried about?

The fear of failure often weighs you down and prevents you from giving your best to the situation at hand. Why would you want to cripple your own chances of success with negative thoughts in your own imagination?

While giving an exam, your focus should merely be on answering the question in front of you.

Stop thinking about the outcome of the exam and worries about the future. The worst-case scenario exercise has already been performed. You have logically arrived at the conclusion that things can never be as bad as you can imagine them to be. By focusing purely on the exam question, you increase your chances of solving it correctly.

My sole aim while attempting a question, is to arrive at the correct answer. If I am successful in doing so, excellent!

Otherwise, shrug it off, wipe your mind clean, and move on!

My favourite line while facing any situation in life is this: "This too shall pass!"

A highly philosophical line, it serves both optimists and pessimists.

If I am facing a lot of success, I should not let it get to my head. I should savour the positive feeling, but move on to better things in life.

If I am facing a lot of failure, I must not take it to heart. I must learn from my failures and move on to better things in life.

How to Stay Motivated Under Exam Pressure: A Guide for Indian Students in Std 12

The 12th standard is undoubtedly one of the most crucial years in a student's academic life. It is a time filled with great expectations, excitement, but also, an overwhelming amount of pressure. Students in India face the enormous challenge of preparing for both their school board exams and college entrance exams. The two-fold pressure is enough to make even the most dedicated student feel like they are juggling flaming torches while riding a unicycle.

It's no surprise that motivation becomes a major concern. The desire to do well is there, but the constant stress, long hours of studying, and the looming uncertainty about the future can cause even the most determined students to question their abilities and commitment. So, how can you stay motivated when the going gets tough?

This chapter will provide practical advice and tips on staying motivated during exam preparation, drawing on the challenges that Indian students face during their 12th standard year. From setting clear goals to maintaining a healthy balance between study and rest, this guide will help students regain focus, push through the pressure, and emerge victorious in their exams.

The Weight of Expectations

Before diving into how to stay motivated, it is important to understand why motivation becomes such a challenge in the first place. For students in India, particularly those in 12th standard, the pressure can be immense. There is often a strong cultural expectation to excel academically, especially in subjects like Science, Commerce, and Humanities. Parents, relatives, and even teachers frequently remind students of the importance of doing well in board exams and college entrance exams.

"You need to get into a good college if you want a successful career!" This mantra rings in every student's ear, along with the constant reminder that their future will be shaped by the marks they score. And when students have to deal with the simultaneous demands of preparing for both school board exams and entrance exams for various courses (such as JEE for engineering, NEET for medicine, or CLAT for law), it's easy to see why they might feel crushed under the weight of these expectations.

There's no denying that the competition is fierce. With so many students vying for limited spots in prestigious colleges, the fear of failure looms large. It's a common feeling among students that if they don't perform well, they won't be able to live up to the dreams and expectations of their families, which can make staying motivated extremely difficult.

The Road to Motivation: Setting Realistic Goals

The key to staying motivated under exam pressure lies in setting realistic, achievable goals. It's easy to become overwhelmed by the sheer scale of what needs to be done, but breaking down the workload into manageable chunks can make it feel more attainable.

Start by defining your end goal. What do you want to achieve by the end of the year? Whether it's scoring high marks in your board exams, cracking your entrance exams, or securing a spot in a particular college, identifying the ultimate goal is crucial for staying on track. Once your big goal is set, it's time to break it down into smaller, more specific targets. Instead of thinking, **"I need to study all of chemistry today,"** break it down to something more actionable, like, **"I will finish Chapter 1 and solve 20 practice questions today."**

When students set realistic goals, they feel a sense of accomplishment after completing each task, which keeps them motivated. It's like running a marathon; you can't focus on the finish line the entire time. Instead, focus on reaching the next milestone, and before you know it, you will be near the finish line.

Time Management: The Secret Weapon

One of the most effective ways to stay motivated is through proper time management. Time management is not just about being busy, but about being productive with the time you have. A lack of time management leads to procrastination, which in turn fuels stress and makes motivation even harder to maintain.

A well-structured timetable is your best friend in times of exam pressure. When preparing for both school and entrance exams, it is essential to have a timetable that allocates time for each subject. But remember, the key is balance. Don't overload your schedule with hours of study without breaks. Just as a car needs fuel to keep going, your brain needs rest to function optimally.

The Pomodoro Technique — studying for 25 minutes and taking a 5-minute break — can be particularly useful for maintaining focus and motivation. After four Pomodoro sessions, take a longer break to recharge. This technique prevents burnout, keeps your mind fresh, and provides short bursts of productivity.

Additionally, don't forget to prioritize your health. When your body feels good, your mind feels good. Make sure to schedule time for exercise, sleep, and relaxation. These breaks from your studies will help you feel refreshed and motivated when you return to your books.

Staying Positive: The Power of a Positive Mindset

One of the biggest challenges students face during exam preparation is maintaining a positive mindset. With the amount of information to learn and the increasing pressure, it is easy to succumb to negativity. Thoughts like **"I'll never be able to finish this,"** or **"What if I fail?"** can paralyze a student's motivation.

However, cultivating a positive attitude can work wonders for boosting motivation. Positive self-talk, where students replace negative thoughts with empowering ones, can go a long way. Instead of thinking, **"I'm terrible at math,"** try thinking, **"I can improve my math skills with consistent practice."**

A powerful strategy is to celebrate small victories along the way. Every time you complete a chapter or a set of practice questions, take a moment to acknowledge your hard work. This helps in building momentum and reinforces the belief that success is attainable. Remind yourself that every step you take brings you closer to your goal.

Managing Stress and Pressure

Stress is inevitable during exam preparation, but it is important to manage it rather than let it consume you. The first step is recognizing the signs of stress. If you find yourself constantly anxious, unable to sleep, or losing focus, it's time to take a step back and reassess.

One way to manage stress is by practicing mindfulness. Meditation, deep breathing exercises, or yoga can help clear the mind, reduce stress, and improve focus. Even spending a few minutes in the morning practicing mindfulness can have a profound impact on how you approach your studies for the rest of the day.

It's also important to avoid self-comparison. Many students fall into the trap of comparing themselves with others, especially when everyone is studying hard around them. **"If they can do it, why can't I?"** becomes a dangerous thought that leads to unnecessary stress. Focus on your own progress and don't worry about what others are doing. Everyone has their own pace, and it's important to recognize and respect that.

In moments of stress, it's also helpful to talk to someone — whether it's a friend, family member, or mentor. Sometimes, simply voicing your concerns can lift a weight off your shoulders.

Embracing Support from Parents and Mentors

In India, where academic pressure is often compounded by parental expectations, it's crucial to have the support of your family. Parents play a vital role in keeping students motivated, but it's essential that this support is positive and understanding. Rather than pushing students to achieve high marks out of fear of failure, parents should foster an environment of encouragement.

Regularly communicate with your parents and mentors about your progress. Share your goals, your challenges, and ask for advice when you feel stuck. A little reassurance can go a long way. **"You're doing great, just keep going"** is often all it takes to reignite motivation.

Mentors or teachers who provide constructive feedback and guide students through difficult concepts are also a great source of motivation. They can provide perspective, offer study tips, and help students stay on track.

Avoiding Burnout: Take Time for Yourself

Amid the hustle and bustle of exam preparation, it is easy to neglect personal well-being. But taking care of yourself is paramount to maintaining motivation. While it's important to work hard, it's just as important to take breaks and do things that relax your mind.

Engage in hobbies, watch a movie, read a book, or hang out with friends — anything that helps you unwind and recharge. Taking time for yourself doesn't mean you're wasting time. On the contrary, it refreshes you and makes you more productive when you return to your studies. A well-rested and mentally clear mind will always perform better than one that is burned out from overwork.

Conclusion

Staying motivated under the intense pressure of preparing for both school board exams and college entrance exams is no easy feat. The stress, anxiety, and sense of overwhelming responsibility can make even the most disciplined students question their abilities. But with the right strategies in place, it is possible to stay motivated, focused, and balanced.

Set realistic goals, manage your time effectively, stay positive, and make sure to take care of your mental and physical health. Remember that success doesn't come from working endlessly without breaks or overburdening yourself with stress. It comes from a balanced approach to preparation — one where you focus on small wins, acknowledge progress, and keep sight of your ultimate goals.

With hard work, determination, and a motivated mindset, students can conquer the challenges that come their way. And as they say, **"The harder you work for something, the greater you'll feel when you achieve it."** So, put in the effort, stay motivated, and the results will follow.

Managing Stress and Staying Mentally Healthy During Exam Time: A Guide for Indian Students in Std 12 Preparing for Entrance Exams

Exam time. It's a phase that makes most students in India feel like they're on a never-ending treadmill—constantly running, but always feeling like they're falling behind. The pressure to perform well in the board exams, coupled with the demand of preparing for entrance exams like JEE, NEET, CLAT, and more, can feel overwhelming. If you're a student in Std 12, you're no stranger to stress. Every day seems like a race against time, and the pressure only builds as the exams approach. But here's the thing—stress doesn't have to be your enemy. In fact, with the right approach, you can manage stress and come out stronger on the other side, both mentally and physically.

The truth is, a certain amount of stress is inevitable during exam time. The key lies in managing it effectively. In this article, we'll explore how you can stay mentally healthy, manage stress, and remain focused while juggling board exams and entrance exam preparations. By adopting some practical strategies, you can keep the stress at bay and approach your exams with a calm and positive mindset.

Understanding the Stress Trap

Before diving into solutions, it's essential to understand what stress actually is. Stress is your body's natural response to a challenge or demand. In small doses, stress can motivate you to study harder and perform better. However, when stress becomes chronic, it can impair your ability to focus, cause physical symptoms like headaches or sleep disturbances, and even affect your overall well-being.

For students in Std 12 preparing for entrance exams, stress is often triggered by the constant race against the clock, the competition, and the fear of not living up to their own or their parents' expectations.

You may find yourself staring at textbooks late into the night, trying to cover everything, only to feel like there's always more to learn. There's the constant anxiety of wondering whether you're doing enough or if you're falling behind. This mental strain is common among Indian students during exam season, but it doesn't have to break you.

1. **Prioritize and Organize**

    When you have mountains of study material to get through and countless subjects to cover, it's easy to feel like you're drowning. The trick to managing stress starts with organizing your tasks in a manageable way.

    Make a Study Plan:

    One of the best ways to keep stress at bay is to create a study plan that works for you. A well-organized timetable is like a roadmap—it helps you see the bigger picture and ensures you're on track.

Break down your day into study blocks. For instance:

- **Morning (8 AM - 12 PM):** Focus on your toughest subject or the one you struggle with the most.

- **Afternoon (1 PM - 4 PM):** Work on revision, practice problems, and mock tests.

- **Evening (5 PM - 8 PM):** Lighter subjects or subjects you're more confident in.

  In between study sessions, ensure that you take regular breaks. They can be small (5-10 minutes) but help in clearing your head and preventing burnout.

Set Realistic Goals:

While it's tempting to think you can conquer the entire syllabus in a week, setting unrealistic goals only adds to your stress. Instead, set achievable daily and weekly goals. Prioritize based on what's most important—your board exams and entrance exams are equally important, but you may need to adjust your focus as the dates draw closer.

Use the Pomodoro Technique:

The Pomodoro Technique is a time management method where you work for 25 minutes and then take a 5-minute break.

After every four sessions, take a longer break of 15-20 minutes. This technique is proven to enhance focus and productivity, making sure that you're working efficiently while avoiding burnout.

2. **Stay Physically Active**

Physical activity is often the last thing on a student's mind during exam season, but it's one of the most important ways to relieve stress. Exercise releases endorphins, chemicals in the brain that act as natural mood boosters. Even something as simple as a 30-minute walk can help clear your mind, boost your mood, and keep you physically energized.

Incorporate Exercise into Your Routine:

Whether it's yoga, walking, jogging, or even dancing to your favourite songs—getting your body moving can refresh your mind and help improve concentration. You don't need to engage in intense workouts, but a regular activity can work wonders. Many students find that doing stretches in the morning or evening not only helps relieve stress but also improves their focus during study sessions.

Mindfulness and Yoga:

Yoga and mindfulness meditation are excellent ways to manage stress and calm your mind. Simple breathing exercises or guided meditation can help lower anxiety and restore your mental energy. Just

15 minutes of meditation daily can make a world of difference in your mental clarity and emotional stability.

3. **Don't Sacrifice Sleep**

In the race to finish the syllabus, it's common for students to give up sleep in favour of extra study hours. This may seem like the solution when the pressure mounts, but depriving yourself of sleep is like running a car without fuel—it might get you somewhere, but not for long.

The Importance of Rest:

Sleep is crucial for memory consolidation. Your brain needs time to process and retain the information you've studied. Lack of sleep not only hinders your ability to retain information but also negatively impacts your mood and concentration.

On average, teenagers need around 7-8 hours of sleep every night. Avoid late-night cramming sessions, as they can lead to fatigue and a drop in cognitive performance. Aim to study during your peak focus hours and make sure you're giving your body and mind enough rest.

Healthy Sleep Habits:

- Keep a consistent sleep schedule.
- Avoid caffeine or heavy meals close to bedtime.
- Unwind by reading or listening to calming music before sleeping.

Remember, "Early to bed, early to rise" is more than just an old adage; it's essential for your mental health and exam success.

4. **Stay Positive and Focus on Your 'Why'**

The pressure of Std 12 exams can often feel suffocating, and it's easy to lose sight of why you're doing it all. When stress gets the better of you, it's essential to reconnect with your purpose.

Remember Your Goals:

Take a moment each day to reflect on why you want to do well in your exams. Whether it's to get into your dream college, pursue a career in engineering, medicine, or law, or simply to make your parents proud—keeping the end goal in mind can provide you with the motivation you need to push through tough times.

Practice Positive Affirmations:

Positive thinking can shift your mindset and keep you focused on what you can control. When anxiety or negative thoughts creep in, counter them with positive affirmations. Tell yourself, "I have prepared well," "I am capable," or "I will do my best." These simple statements can do wonders for your mental state.

5. **Reach Out for Support**

As much as we'd like to think we can handle everything ourselves, it's okay to ask for help. Whether it's from a teacher, a friend, or your family, don't hesitate to talk about the pressures you're feeling. Talking things through with someone can provide clarity, offer a fresh perspective, or simply make you feel less alone in this journey.

Talk to Your Parents:

Indian students often feel immense pressure from their parents during exam time. While it's important to meet their expectations, it's equally important to express how you're feeling. A calm and honest conversation with your parents can ease some of the pressure and help them understand what you're going through.

Consult a Mentor or Counsellor:

If the stress feels overwhelming, consider talking to a school counsellor or a mentor. They can offer you valuable advice on stress management and provide emotional support during exam preparation.

6. **Maintain a Balanced Diet**

It's easy to fall into unhealthy eating habits during exam season. Fast food and caffeinated drinks might seem like quick fixes to get you through long study sessions, but these can spike your stress levels and affect your focus.

Eat Nutrient-Rich Foods:

Ensure that your diet includes plenty of fruits, vegetables, whole grains, and proteins. Foods like nuts, leafy greens, and berries are known to support brain function and keep your energy levels steady throughout the day.

Stay Hydrated:

Don't forget to drink plenty of water. Dehydration can lead to fatigue, headaches, and impaired concentration.

As the saying goes, "You are what you eat"—so fuel your body with healthy food to keep your mind sharp.

Conclusion: You've Got This!

The road to exam success is filled with challenges, but managing stress doesn't have to be one of them. By staying organized, maintaining a balanced routine, taking care of your physical and mental health, and leaning on your support system, you can face exam season with confidence and resilience. Remember, it's not about the pressure; it's about how you manage it. Keep calm, take it one step at a time, and stay focused on your goals. With the right mindset, the finish line will be within reach, and success will be yours to claim.

PART 5: PARENTS

Dealing With Parental Pressure: A Guide for Indian Students Preparing for Board and Entrance Exams

The 12th standard is often regarded as the most significant year in a student's academic journey. It is a time when everything seems to hinge on their performance: school board exams, college entrance exams, and the expectations of parents, teachers, and peers. Among all the pressures students face, the one that often weighs heaviest is the pressure from parents.

For many Indian students, parental pressure is a constant companion, pushing them to excel in exams, get top marks, and secure admission to prestigious colleges. Parents, in their genuine desire to see their children succeed, sometimes create an environment that feels more stressful than supportive. While this pressure can be a source of motivation for some, it can be overwhelming for others, leading to anxiety, burnout, and self-doubt.

In this article, we'll explore how students can deal with the pressure from parents, especially when preparing for both school board exams and entrance exams for competitive courses like engineering, medicine, law, or management. This is a tough year for most students, but with the right mindset and strategies, they can manage their academic responsibilities while maintaining their mental and emotional well-being.

Understanding the Roots of Parental Pressure

Before we dive into how to deal with parental pressure, it's essential to understand where this pressure comes from. Indian parents, especially in traditional families, place a significant amount of emphasis on academic success. **"Education is the key to a bright future"** is a mantra that has been passed down through generations. This belief, combined with the social status associated with professional careers like engineering and medicine, leads parents to view academic achievement as a direct pathway to success and financial security.

In a country like India, where the competition is fierce and opportunities limited, parents often feel that their children need to perform exceptionally well in their board exams and entrance exams to stand a chance at securing a good future. This creates a high level of expectation. They might push their children to study relentlessly, sometimes crossing the line between encouragement and pressure. The fear of their children falling behind in a competitive environment can make them more vocal, demanding, and controlling.

"If you don't get into a good college, where will you go?" This question is asked time and again, and it can feel like a looming cloud hanging over a student's head. The pressure to meet these expectations can leave students feeling isolated, frustrated, and uncertain about how to balance their own aspirations with their parents' dreams for them.

The Emotional Toll of Parental Pressure

The emotional toll that parental pressure can take on students is significant. For one, it creates an environment where students feel they are constantly being judged based on their academic performance. Every test score, every assignment, and every entrance exam becomes a benchmark of their worth. The stress of living up to these standards can lead to mental health issues like anxiety, depression, and burnout.

Additionally, the comparison game is often a painful reality. If a student's sibling, cousin, or friend is excelling academically, it can add another layer of pressure. **"Why can't you be like your cousin who topped the board exams?"** These comparisons often make students feel inadequate, regardless of how hard they're working.

Moreover, the looming deadlines for both board exams and entrance exams add to the sense of urgency and pressure. Students are expected to study continuously, and the concept of taking breaks or doing something relaxing can be dismissed as unnecessary or even indulgent. This can lead to a sense of being trapped in a cycle of endless studying, where there is no time for anything else.

The Struggle of Managing Expectations

While most parents have the best intentions, their overwhelming expectations can unintentionally create an environment of fear and resentment. For many students, it feels like they are living for others rather than for themselves. The question that looms large is: **"What if I don't meet my parents' expectations?"**

However, it's essential for students to remember that their parents are coming from a place of concern. They want their children to succeed because they love them and want them to have a better life than they had. But this doesn't mean that students should shoulder all the burden alone.

How to Deal with Parental Pressure: Practical Tips

1. **Communicate Openly and Honestly**

   One of the most effective ways to deal with parental pressure is to communicate openly with your parents about how you're feeling. If you're overwhelmed or struggling with the workload, don't bottle it up. Express your concerns calmly and let them know how their expectations are affecting you.

   "I understand that you want the best for me, but I'm feeling stressed and need some time to recharge."

   Such conversations can help your parents understand your emotional state, and they might be more inclined to offer support rather than pressure.

2. **Set Realistic Expectations Together**

   Sometimes, students set unrealistic goals for themselves, partly due to the pressure from parents. Have a conversation with your parents about what is achievable based on your strengths and weaknesses.

This way, you can align their expectations with what is realistically possible.

If you're not a fan of biology and have no interest in pursuing medicine, but your parents keep pushing you towards it, have an honest conversation about your career aspirations and what you truly want. Help them understand that pushing you towards a path that doesn't interest you will not help you perform well.

3. **Take Control of Your Schedule**

Often, parental pressure stems from the desire for students to make the most of their time. While it's important to study hard, it's equally crucial to have a balanced schedule. Take charge of your timetable and ensure that it includes not only study hours but also time for relaxation and hobbies.

The key to surviving the pressure is knowing when to push yourself and when to pull back. Overloading yourself with study hours can lead to burnout. Set your own goals and allow some flexibility for breaks, exercise, and socializing, which are just as important for maintaining mental health.

4. **Focus on Self-Care**

Under pressure, students often forget to take care of themselves physically and emotionally. The long hours of studying can lead to exhaustion, both mentally and physically. It's essential to listen to your body and take care of yourself.

Sleep, eat well, and take regular breaks. Engage in activities like sports, reading, or even spending time with friends to refresh your mind. All work and no play can lead to stress, and that's when motivation dips. Remember, a healthy body supports a healthy mind.

5. **Seek Guidance from Mentors and Teachers**

Parents might have high expectations, but so do teachers and mentors. Seek guidance from teachers who are willing to offer practical tips for exam preparation. Teachers are often more understanding than parents and can provide useful advice on managing time, prioritizing subjects, and navigating stress.

Mentors can also help you gain perspective. They have often been in your shoes and can offer advice on how they handled similar pressures. A mentor might provide the reassurance you need that you are not alone in this journey.

6. **Learn to Say No When Necessary**

Sometimes, students need to draw boundaries. If parents are pushing you too hard or giving you too many tasks, it's okay to say no. Be respectful but firm about your limitations. If a specific request or demand feels unreasonable, explain your point of view clearly.

"I can't attend another extra class today because I need time to revise." Respecting your own limits is crucial to maintaining a balanced life. Remember that it's okay to set limits on what you can handle.

7. **Celebrate Small Wins**

Don't wait for the final exam results to celebrate your hard work. Acknowledge and celebrate small wins along the way, whether it's mastering a challenging topic, finishing a mock test, or staying focused for a week without getting distracted. These small victories will not only boost your confidence but also provide a much-needed break from the constant cycle of studying.

When parents see the effort you're putting in, they'll appreciate the progress you're making, and this can ease some of their expectations.

8. **Find a Support Network**

Surround yourself with friends, family members, or classmates who understand what you're going through. Having a support network is invaluable. Sharing your concerns, talking about your struggles, and offering advice to each other can provide comfort and perspective. You're not alone in this.

9. **Focus on the Bigger Picture**

Finally, it's important to keep in mind the bigger picture. Your life is more than just exams. While the 12th standard may feel like the most important year of your life, it's only one chapter in your entire journey. Parents need to be reminded that success in life is not measured solely by marks on an exam paper but by happiness, self-growth, and personal fulfilment.

Acknowledging your own goals and passions will help you stay grounded in the midst of external pressures.

Conclusion

Dealing with parental pressure is never easy, especially for students preparing for school board exams and entrance exams simultaneously. But by communicating openly with your parents, setting realistic goals, and prioritizing self-care, you can strike a balance between meeting expectations and staying true to yourself. Always remember that your worth is not determined by your exam results, and the journey you are on is just as important as the destination.

If you are ever feeling overwhelmed, don't hesitate to reach out for support from mentors, friends, or counsellors. It's okay to ask for help and take a step back when you need it. The most important thing is to stay grounded, stay focused, and keep moving forward one step at a time.

Why Indian Parents Are Obsessed with Their Children Studying Engineering and Medicine After Completing School: A Story of Pressure, Expectations, and Alternate Paths

In a small town nestled in the heart of India, there lived a young boy named Narayan. Like most Indian children, Narayan was bright, ambitious, and always eager to please his parents. From a young age, his parents made it abundantly clear that the only acceptable career paths for him were either engineering or medicine. The reasons for this were simple, yet deeply ingrained in the cultural fabric of Indian society. These two fields—engineering and medicine—were seen as prestigious, financially secure, and the hallmark of success. As Narayan stood on the cusp of finishing school and deciding his future, he couldn't shake off the constant pressure he felt from his family and peers.

Narayan's story is not unique. It reflects the experiences of millions of students across India who face the immense weight of expectations from their families when it comes to career choices. The obsession with engineering and medicine in India is deeply rooted in tradition, societal perceptions, and a host of practical considerations. Yet, as we delve deeper into this issue, it becomes clear that while engineering and medicine are indeed appropriate and promising career paths for some, they may not necessarily be the right choice for everyone. In this article, we will explore why Indian parents are so fixated on these two fields, why this obsession might be appropriate for some but not for others, and what alternative career paths can offer a fulfilling future.

The Roots of the Obsession: Tradition and Societal Pressure

To understand why Indian parents are obsessed with engineering and medicine, we must first examine the socio-cultural landscape that has shaped these preferences. In India, family and social approval are of paramount importance. Career choices are often viewed not just as a personal decision but as a reflection of the family's social status and prestige. From an early age, children are conditioned to believe that certain professions—especially those in engineering and medicine—are synonymous with respect, success, and security.

Historically, India's education system has placed a strong emphasis on technical and scientific knowledge. Engineering and medicine were seen as fields that offered not only intellectual rigor but also financial stability. The rise of the IT sector in the 1990s further solidified the idea that engineering, particularly computer science and software engineering, was a lucrative and secure profession. Similarly, medicine has always been viewed as a noble profession, one that offers respect in society and the potential for a stable income.

The fixation with these fields is also driven by peer pressure. In many communities, parents often compete with each other in terms of their children's achievements. If a neighbour's child becomes a doctor or an engineer, it is often viewed as a point of pride, and other parents may push their own children to follow suit. This cycle perpetuates the obsession with these two fields, as parents fear that their children will be left behind if they choose a less conventional career path.

Why Engineering and Medicine Make Sense for Some

For certain students, the pressure to pursue engineering or medicine may be justified. These fields are well-established and offer several benefits, both tangible and intangible. Let's look at why engineering and medicine may indeed be suitable career choices for some individuals.

Engineering: A Path to Innovation and Financial Security

Engineering, particularly in disciplines like computer science, electrical, and mechanical engineering, offers immense potential for those with a passion for technology and problem-solving. India's booming tech industry, which includes global giants like Infosys, TCS, Wipro, and a rapidly growing startup ecosystem, provides numerous job opportunities for talented engineers. Engineering is often viewed as a gateway to the modern world, where innovations in technology, robotics, artificial intelligence, and software are shaping the future.

For students who have a strong affinity for mathematics, physics, and technology, engineering can be an ideal path. It provides the intellectual challenges and rewards that come with solving real-world problems and developing new technologies. Moreover, engineering can also offer financial security, as top engineering graduates often land well-paying jobs at global companies, or even go on to create their own successful startups. For students like Narayan, who are passionate about coding, designing, or building things, engineering can provide a fulfilling and prosperous career.

Medicine: A Noble and Respected Profession

Similarly, medicine has long been considered one of the most prestigious and respected professions in India. Being a doctor is not only about diagnosing illnesses and treating patients—it is seen as a vocation that comes with a sense of duty to society. Doctors are often revered as lifesavers, and the profession commands a high level of respect. Furthermore, medicine offers the potential for financial stability and success, especially for those who specialize in fields like surgery, dermatology, or cardiology.

For students who have a genuine interest in biology, anatomy, and the healthcare industry, medicine can be an ideal choice. It offers an intellectually stimulating and rewarding career, where the work directly impacts people's lives. Moreover, the opportunities to specialize and practice medicine in diverse settings—be it in government hospitals, private practice, or global health organizations—make it a versatile and globally recognized career option.

The Dark Side: Why It's Not the Right Fit for Everyone

Despite the merits of engineering and medicine, not every student is cut out for these fields. There are several reasons why the obsession with these two professions can be detrimental, both for students and for society as a whole.

Lack of Passion and Interest

The most fundamental problem with the engineering and medicine obsession is that not every student has a genuine passion or aptitude for these fields. Many students are pushed into these careers by their parents, often without considering their own interests or inclinations. The result is a generation of young people who are studying subjects they have no real interest in, leading to burnout, dissatisfaction, and sometimes even failure.

Take, for example, Narayan. While he had always been good at science, he had no real love for engineering or medicine. What he truly enjoyed was writing, creating stories, and understanding how the human mind worked. But the constant pressure to follow the "safe" route of engineering or medicine led him to feel trapped in a career that wasn't his own. This lack of passion for his chosen field left him feeling disengaged and disconnected, a fate that many students face when their true aspirations are sidelined by parental pressure.

Overcrowding in Popular Fields

Another issue with the obsession with engineering and medicine is that both fields have become overcrowded. The number of engineering colleges in India has skyrocketed in recent years, leading to an oversupply of engineers. While there is still demand for skilled engineers, the sheer number of graduates each year means that many engineers struggle to find jobs that match their qualifications.

The medical field faces similar challenges. While India is in dire need of more healthcare professionals, the number of medical graduates far exceeds the demand in some areas. This leads to intense competition, job scarcity in certain regions, and the growing influence of private healthcare, where only the most prestigious institutions can guarantee high-paying roles.

Mental Health Impact

The pressure to succeed in engineering and medicine can take a toll on students' mental health. The intense competition, long hours of studying, and constant pressure to perform often lead to stress, anxiety, and depression. In a country where failure is often seen as shameful, many students feel isolated and inadequate when they struggle to keep up with the rigorous demands of these fields.

Narayan, like many other students, faced a period of mental exhaustion. The constant push to perform well in both his board exams and entrance exams left him with little time to relax, explore his interests, or pursue hobbies. This relentless pressure, combined with the fear of disappointing his family, created a toxic cycle of stress and self-doubt.

Alternate Career Paths: Broadening Horizons

While engineering and medicine are excellent career choices for some, they are not the only paths to success.

In recent years, there has been a growing recognition of the value of alternate career options that cater to a wider range of interests and talents. Let's take a look at some of these alternate career paths that students like Narayan can explore.

Business Management and Entrepreneurship

One of the most popular alternatives to engineering and medicine is business management. With the rise of the startup culture and the booming e-commerce industry, business management has become a highly sought-after career option. Top business schools like the Indian Institutes of Management (IIMs) offer world-class education in management, equipping students with the skills to become successful entrepreneurs, marketers, financial analysts, and leaders in the corporate world.

Entrepreneurship, in particular, offers an exciting and dynamic career path for students who are passionate about innovation and problem-solving. With the right training and mindset, students can create their own businesses and drive change in various industries. For students who are more inclined towards creativity and leadership rather than technical subjects, business management and entrepreneurship offer a world of possibilities.

Law

Law is another field that has gained immense popularity in recent years, especially with the growth of corporate law, intellectual property law, and human rights law. Law offers students a chance to engage with society, advocate for justice, and make a significant impact in the legal system.

Prestigious law schools like the National Law Universities (NLUs) offer excellent education and open doors to high-paying legal careers in law firms, corporate sectors, or the judiciary.

Design, Arts, and Humanities

For students with a creative bent of mind, fields like design, fine arts, literature, and humanities offer exciting career prospects. Graphic design, animation, interior design, fashion design, and architecture are just a few of the fields that have seen significant growth in recent years. These fields not only allow students to express their creativity but also offer well-paying career opportunities in both the public and private sectors.

Additionally, students who are passionate about history, literature, psychology, or sociology can pursue careers in academia, research, journalism, or social work. These fields may not always be as glamorous as engineering or medicine, but they offer a sense of fulfilment and purpose that can be deeply satisfying.

Hospitality and Tourism Management

Hospitality and tourism management is another growing sector in India, particularly with the rise of domestic and international tourism. Students who are interested in this field can pursue degrees in hotel management, tourism, and event planning. With India being one of the most popular tourist destinations in the world, careers in hospitality offer the opportunity to work in dynamic, fast-paced environments while interacting with people from diverse backgrounds.

Conclusion: The Key Is Balance and Understanding

As we reflect on Narayan's story, it becomes clear that the obsession with engineering and medicine in India is both understandable and problematic. While these fields can be appropriate and rewarding for some students, they are not a one-size-fits-all solution. Every student is unique, and career choices should be made based on individual strengths, interests, and aspirations.

Parents must recognize that their children's happiness and success lie in pursuing careers that align with their passions, not just in following societal expectations. Encouraging students to explore alternate career paths like business, law, design, or hospitality can open doors to new opportunities, allowing them to find fulfilment and success in their own way.

The key is balance. Parents should support their children in making informed decisions, based on their own interests and abilities, rather than pushing them down a path that may not suit them. It's time for India to embrace a more holistic view of education, where success is defined by individual growth, happiness, and the pursuit of one's true calling—not just by the traditional markers of engineering and medicine.

GLOSSARY

AICTE

The ALL-INDIA COUNCIL FOR TECHNICAL EDUCATION (AICTE) is a statutory body, and a national-level council for technical education, under the Department of Higher Education. Established in November 1945 first as an advisory body, which was given statutory status by an Act of Parliament in 1987, the AICTE is responsible for proper planning and coordinated development of the technical education and management education system in India.

AIIMS

ALL INDIA INSTITUTE OF MEDICAL SCIENCES

The All-India Institutes of Medical Sciences (AIIMS) is a group of autonomous government public medical universities of higher education under the jurisdiction of Ministry of Health and Family Welfare, Government of India. These institutes have been declared by an Act of Parliament as Institutes of National Importance. AIIMS New Delhi, the forerunner institute, was established in 1956.

AILET

The ALL-INDIA LAW ENTRANCE TEST is a national level entrance exam conducted by National Law University Delhi for admission to its law programs.

CAT

The Common Admission Test (CAT) is a computer-based test for admission in graduate management programs. The test consists of three sections: Verbal Ability and Reading Comprehension (VARC), Data Interpretation and Logical Reasoning (DILR) and Quantitative Ability (QA). The exam is taken online over a period of three hours, with one hour per section.

CLAT

The COMMON LAW ADMISSION TEST (CLAT) is a national level entrance exam for admissions to undergraduate (UG) and postgraduate (PG) law programmes offered by National Law Universities in India (except NLU Delhi).

CLAT is organized by the Consortium of National Law Universities, comprising representative universities.

Several affiliate universities and organisations also use the CLAT exam for admissions and recruitment respectively.

CUET

The COMMON UNIVERSITY ENTRANCE TEST (CUET), formerly Central Universities Common Entrance

Test (CUCET) is a standardised test in India conducted by the National Testing Agency at various levels—CUET (UG), CUET (PG), and CUET (PhD), for admission to undergraduate, postgraduate, and doctorate programmes in Central Universities and other participating institutes. It is also accepted by number of other State Universities and Deemed universities in India

IIM

INDIAN INSTITUTE OF MANAGEMENT

The Indian Institutes of Management (IIMs) are Centrally Funded Business Schools for management offering undergraduate, postgraduate, doctoral and executive programmes along with some additional courses in the field of business administration.

IIT

INDIAN INSTITUTE OF TECHNOLOGY

The Indian Institutes of Technology (IITs) are a network of engineering and technology institutions in India. Established in 1950, they are under the purview of the Ministry of Education of the Indian Government and are governed by the Institutes of Technology Act, 1961. The Act refers to them as Institutes of National Importance and lays down their powers, duties, and framework for governance as the country's premier institutions in the field of technology

IPMAT

The INTEGRATED PROGRAM IN MANAGEMENT ADMISSION TEST is conducted by the Indian Institute of Management (IIM) Indore for admission to its five-year integrated management program, which combines a Bachelor's and Master's degree. IPMAT is a national-level entrance exam held annually.

The scores of the IPMAT held by IIM Indore are also considered by other institutes such as IIM Ranchi and Nirma University.

There is a separate IPMAT conducted by IIM Rohtak for admission to their five-year integrated programme.

JEE

The JOINT ENTRANCE EXAMINATION, JEE (Main) is an entrance exam conducted by the National Testing Agency for admission to various engineering programs.

The JEE comprises two papers. Paper 1 is conducted for admission to Undergraduate Engineering Programs (B.E/B.Tech.) at NITs, IIITs, other Centrally Funded Technical Institutions (CFTIs), and Institutions/ Universities funded/recognized by participating State Governments.

JEE (Main) is also an eligibility test for JEE (Advanced), which is conducted for admission to IITs.

Paper 2 is conducted for admission to B. Arch and B. Planning courses in the country.

JIPMAT

JOINT INTEGRATED PROGRAMME IN MANAGEMENT ADMISSION TEST is a national level test conducted by NTA for admission to Five Year

Integrated Programme in Management at IIM Bodh Gaya and IIM Jammu.

NEET

NATIONAL ELIGIBILITY CUM ENTRANCE TEST (NEET (UG)) is conducted by National Testing Agency (NTA), as a common and uniform National Eligibility-cum-Entrance Test [(NEET (UG)] for admission to undergraduate medical education in all medical institutions.

Similarly, as per Section 14 of the National Commission for Indian System of Medicine Act, 2020, there is a uniform NEET (UG) for admission to undergraduate courses in each of the disciplines i.e. BAMS, BUMS, and BSMS courses of the Indian System of Medicine in all Medical Institutions governed under this Act.

NEET (UG) is also applicable to admission to BHMS course as per National Commission for Homeopathy Act, 2020.

NIT

NATIONAL INSTITUTE OF TECHNOLOGY

The National Institutes of Technology (NITs) are centrally funded technical institutes under the ownership of the Ministry of Education, Government of India. They are governed by the National Institutes of Technology, Science Education, and Research Act, 2007, which declared them institutions of national importance and laid down their powers, duties, and framework for governance. The act lists 32 NITs. Each NIT is autonomous and linked to the others through a common council known as the Council of NITSER, which oversees their administration. All NITs are funded by the Government of India.

NLU

NATIONAL LAW UNIVERSITY

National Law Universities (NLU) are public law schools in India, founded pursuant to the second-generation reforms for legal education sought to be implemented by the Bar Council of India. The first NLU was the National Law School of India University aka NLS/NLU Bangalore which admitted its first batch in 1988. Since then, most of the states in India have NLUs.

SLAT

The Symbiosis Law Admission Test (SLAT) opens doors to Symbiosis law institutes across the country. It is a one-hour, computer-based test designed to test the skills needed to excel in legal education. Programmes offered by institutes of Symbiosis International (Deemed University) have to appear for the common, mandatory Computer Based Test (CBT).

UGC

UNIVERSITY GRANTS COMMISSION is a statutory body under Department of Higher Education, Ministry of Education, Government of India. It was set up in accordance to the UGC Act 1956 and is charged with coordination, determination and maintenance of standards of higher education in India. It provides recognition to universities in India, and disbursements of funds to such recognized universities and colleges.

Pomodoro Technique

In the late 1980s, the Italian Francesco Cirillo invented the most effective time-management method: **The Pomodoro Technique**. He experimented with several time management tools to find out the best way to get things done. He used his tomato-shaped kitchen timer for dividing his tasks into 25-minute work intervals and five-minute breaks.

While practicing it, he found out that he was able to complete tasks more effectively than before. On that observation, he concluded that if you divide a large task into small manageable time units then it becomes easy to complete it. Later on, he named this method after his kitchen timer which was shaped like a Pomodoro which means "tomato" in Italian.